THE POWER OF BEING

FOR PEOPLE WHO DO TOO MUCH!

by

CHRISTIAN R. KOMOR, Psy.D.

Published by
Renegade House Productions
Grand Rapids, Michigan

THE POWER OF BEING FOR PEOPLE WHO DO TOO MUCH

Library of Congress Cataloging in Publication Data

Komor, Christian R., 1959-
    The power of being : for people who do too much! / by
    Christian R. Komor.
        p.   cm.
    Includes bibliographic references.
    1. Workaholism. 2. Workaholics — Rehabilitation. I.
Title.
RC569.5.W67K66   1992
616.85'2 — dc20   92-13568
                                                   CIP

ISBN # 0-9632763-0-1

Publisher: Renegade House Productions
               P.O. Box 6025
               Grand Rapids, Michigan 49516
               (616) 956-7905

DEDICATION

This book is dedicated to my wife, Paulette, with whom I have shared my greatest adventures and with whom I look forward to sharing many more.

CONTENTS

*** Reader: If you are wondering if this book is for
you - see Appendix A . . .

FOREWORD AND ACKNOWLEDGEMENTS

I am glad that you are reading this book. Not just because it feels good as an author to have one's work appreciated, but because of the critical nature of this topic for this generation. Society is having a problem with the way in which we approach the tasks and duties of daily living. The more of us who stop identifying ourselves as "human doings" and start living as the spontaneous human *beings* we were intended to be, the better for everyone. I want to acknowledge you, the reader, for taking steps toward reclaiming that right to be.

As a compulsive doer myself, I should note that, for me, writing is both a pleasure and a danger! Originally this book itself was an unhealthy expression of my own addiction to doing and neglect of my own need to "be". For me, the creative process is at times a balance between release and frenzy — this book was definitely born of the latter! It took me some months of introspection before I could complete this manuscript in a way that was healthy for me and hopefully helpful for you. I hope that, as a reader, you will approach this book in a relaxed and lighthearted manner.

Although it's customary to thank a spouse last, the relationship I have enjoyed over the years with my wife has always been in the forefront of my life in terms of growth, nurturing and challenge. It seems fitting, therefore, that I should thank her first rather than last! For better or for worse, she has offered me more than I can possibly express in crude words. Besides myself, she is the person with whom I am most likely to experience the power of being.

For their many gifts and contributions to my life, and therefore the development of the material in this book, I would like to thank: George E. Lewis, Werner Erhard, Thomas F. Crum, Richard Williams, Everett L. Shostrom, George Leonard, John Denver, Clayton Nalui, Koichi Tohei, Tom Wilkinson, John Friel, John Otterbacher, Daniel Hendrickson, Jerry Van Leeuwen, Roy Welton, Sarah Ash, Daniel Rosen, Elly Brown, Thomas Moore, John Gorka, my many courageous clients, and all my friends in recovery.

Among those who contributed to the actual preparation of this manuscript I would like to especially thank: Paulette Komor, Art Edson, Sally Komor, Christopher Scheil, Gary Wharton, Kim Hayslip, Lori Nash, James McCarthy, and Marion Younghans.

Finally, my warmest thanks and love go to my parents-in-law (the Polish Zen masters of the Northwest Side) and especially my own parents Carl and Sally, and brother Steve who have given me life with plenty of reasons to live (and adventures to go on). Without them I would have had no reason to, or skills with which to explore these issues and thus no solutions to offer you, the reader. Again, words fail to convey the importance and depth of such relationships where only the heart knows all that has passed between.

Christian R. Komor
Grand Rapids, Mich.
October, 1992

THE VOYAGE

A s we look around and within there is evidence everywhere that society is becoming increasingly and dangerously acclimated to what has come to be known as *stress*. Many express unhappiness with the hectic nature of society and the demands that are placed on all of us. We long for the "good old days" when things were simpler and the pace of life was slower. Yet we either feel powerless to make the changes needed to get out of the fast lane, or find that the changes we do make only lead to more things that we need to take care of or accomplish. Life in our times can seem an endless treadmill of work and responsibilities that are no longer fulfilling or nurturing.

The problem that our society is having with work and excessive doing is so pervasive that most of the time it is difficult to see. Compulsive doing, or workaholism, has become part of the *context* in which we live our lives. We have become dangerously acclimated to a level of stress which is unhealthy and places physical health and the natural environment at risk. Efforts to accomplish more and to create a better lifestyle have created a dangerous and contradictory world, where everything is available at the dial of an 800 number, and everything is also at terrible risk. We want it all, but run the risk of losing it all, as we chip away at personal health and the planet's fragile resources. This is the cost and risk of compulsive doing, but it is a legacy we can change.

In working with people in psychotherapy, I frequently hear stories of heroic attempts to do it all, or to make it all work. Bombarded by the media's accounts of successful people who have juggled marriage, children, several tremendously lucrative and rewarding careers, as well as a non-stop social schedule, people wonder why they aren't able to keep up. Yet, in our quieter moments we may also wonder if we want to. For many the image of perfection and achievement created in our culture seems to have taken over, replacing spontaneity, love, and desire with force, effort, and trophies of money and material things.

The purpose of this book is to show you how to move from a life of shoulds, have-tos, and over-commitments to one of spontaneity, satisfaction, and serenity. Each of us has the power to change our *approach* to a stressful world. No matter what the circumstances, there are important changes which can be initiated now, *today*. (both in your perspective of life and the way you approach your environment) that will lead back to a sense of spontaneity, choicefulness, and serenity.

Clearly the demands of the environment have a significant impact upon us, yet we can *choose* how to respond to these pressures. The ability to approach life from an internal perspective of balance and centeredness, is the key to healing from "compulsive doing".

Stress is not just a result of the outside environment, but of how we *react* to and deal with that environment. There are those who, for various reasons, are drawn to a lifestyle that involves excessive amounts of accomplishing, doing, "shoulding" (doing what is "should" be done rather than what is want to be done), and forcing ourselves. If you have found yourself attracted to this book, you may already recognize these qualities to some degree within.

This book will address the tendency to do too much as an actual addiction. The addiction model has been chosen partly because it is descriptive of the process society has fallen into of excessive working while feeling increasingly out of control (like alcoholics with their drinking). This model also helps to understand why some people are more affected by pressures to work and accomplish while others are not. There are those whose backgrounds and experiences set them up to be lured into the fast lane of society and to become stuck there. Again, this is similar to what happens for the alcoholic.

Just as some people are able to drink alcohol without feeling compulsive, there are those who are able to look at society's increasing complexity as a joyful opportunity to experience more and be better, more fulfilled people. Unfortunately, as with alcohol, some people tend to become addicted to the choices, challenges, and complexity of society. Living in present-day America can be like swimming in a pool of alcohol for the alcoholic. It is all too tempting to become carried away, and lose ourselves in the process.

Over the years there have been a variety of other terms used to describe compulsive doing. For example, many compulsive doers can also be described as "workaholics" or as suffering from "hurry sickness". Compulsive doers also may evidence what is known as "Type-A behavior" which is a tendency to engage in a chronic struggle to achieve more and more in less and less time. Psychologists and psychiatrists have traditionally referred to the compulsive doing lifestyle by the term "Obsessive-Compulsive Personality". Each one of these terms describes *essentially the same* compulsive approach to living and working — one that leads directly to high levels of stress and low levels of happiness and spontaneity.

Many have been led to believe that stress is somehow productive, and gets us ahead in life. That belief, as we will see, is a fallacy. In actuality, stress is generally the *opposite* of satisfaction and can act as an addictive *substitute* for the happiness of being that is our birthright. To illustrate, let me tell you a story of one stressed-out fellow.

The winter of 1984, was to become one of the most traumatic I have ever experienced. One night while eating pizza with my wife, I began to have a frightening sense that I was no longer real. I knew that this was actually not the case, but I nonetheless had a troubling sense of detachment and alienation from myself.

In the ocean of life ships sometimes run aground. Sometimes that is exactly what they need to do! In the coming weeks the sensations I had of loss of self expanded into what I can only describe as full-blown anxiety attacks. Without apparent warning I would find myself shaking and sweating, unable to sleep or eat, restless and agitated. I was pursued by a pervasive sense of dread which seemed unconnected to the realities of my life.

Certainly I could have asked for a more relaxing and nurturing work situation. As a Clinical Psychologist at the nation's largest walled prison there were many difficult situations to deal with on a daily basis. Overall, however, things seemed to be going well. I had been married for several years with an income greater than oither of us had anticipated. We lived in a comfortable apartment, both had a number of new and old friends and even subscribed to HBO. I had also done some valuable personal growth work in the past year about which I felt quite accomplished and fulfilled. Yet there were these nagging anxiety attacks.

If asked in 1984, I would have told you I was not having much fun! It was, in fact, a first-hand encounter with the effects of my own addiction to doing. Looking back, however, that time was paradoxically one of the most growthful and healing times in my life. It was also the beginning of eight years of discovery and research that have led to the creation of this book. What I "discovered" was a powerful sense of *being*— a spontaneous and natural way of living in the world that I hope to share with you through this book. (The title of this book occured to me in 1985 while practicing the "Doing Nothing" exercise in Chapter Six.)

Since that time I have had the privilege of working with scores of individuals struggling to find balance in a world which draws us so easily into overworking and overdoing. As humans we so easily lose touch with our own *being*— the person inside of us that knows how to play, be spontaneous, and work because we choose to, not because we are driven to. As both a sufferer and a healer, I have explored the terrain of compulsive doing and emerged with exciting results. This book is my way of sharing with you those personal and professional discoveries.

In participating in the healing process with clients, workshop participants and students, the powerful differences between a life focused on doing and one lived out of a desire to *be* have become apparent. Frequently clients will share with me the amazing changes they have experienced as they work through their compulsive doing. Frequently also, they will share the gratitude they feel toward their former compulsive habits — without which they would never have learned the power of being. As you will see as we journey together through this book, our compulsiveness can lead us to wonderful self-realizations and eventually to a more healthy way of being in our world. In fact, our individual healing can lead to important contributions to the world in general.

This book is written from deep inside the journey that I have been taking. I hope that these words can reach deep inside of you. It is my hope that somewhere in this book, you will find something for yourself — something you have missed out on, something that will assist you in becoming more whole. The journey of healing from compulsive doing is not easy, nor is it simple and straightforward. The addiction to work, accomplishing, and shoulds is part of us that we cannot put aside like a bottle of pills. We must learn to live with and grow through this compulsiveness. We must find a way to befriend it and use it as a catalyst for healing.

That healing voyage begins with the discovery that we have been living in enslavement to the process of accomplishing, doing, and "shoulding". It is about recovery from an addiction to working, achieving, and "being all that you can be" until there is nothing left of the real you to be. The primary purpose of this book is to assist you in charting a course through the difficult waters of obsessive-compulsive doing into the safe harbor of self-ownership, beingness, and spontaneity.

You will notice that throughout this book I continue to liken the journey from compulsive doing to healthy being as a sailing voyage. There are few journeys more ancient and primal that those over water. I believe that the journey out of artificially imposed shoulds and compulsivity and back to our natural state of beingness is likewise one that is very basic to the human condition.

From the Bible through the works of contemporary philosophers and across all major world religions, there runs the idea of loving oneself — of a kingdom of God within. This journey that I am pointing to throughout this book from compulsive doing to healthy being is that same trek back to the self that people have been making since time began.

The difference in our generation is that there is even more at risk as a culture if we refuse the journey. Our fragile ecosystem is sensitive to which of the two states (compulsive doing or healthy being) in which we live our lives. Compulsive doing invariably takes more from our environment than it gives back. Conversely, our current world presents us with special opportunities. More of us have access to the intellectual and physical resources needed to take the journey from doing to being. The greater our suffering from compulsive doing the more energetically we can propel ourselves into healthy being.

Before drawing these introductory remarks to a close three final issues deserve mention. First, some of the suggestions and observations in this book may mislead people to think that I am advocating laziness and sloth. Many of the strategies of healing I suggest *are* directly contradictory to our society's traditional work ethics. It is important for you to understand, however, that I am *not* going to be giving instruction on how to be lazy, shiftless, or selfish. (I, in fact, still put in more work hours than I really should. With several graduate degrees and a private practice I am no stranger to hard work.) This book *is about finding balance* in a society which has become overly focused on work, accomplishing, and doing, *not neglecting* responsibilities or avoiding commitments. We are talking about a return to a more natural state of being where work and play and relationships all have a place and spontaneity is the thread running through each.

Secondly, it is important to note that the concepts and suggestions made in this book are those of this author. This does not mean that they are right for you. On the path to the power of being we each have to find our own course. This is *very* important! Focusing more on what we *should* do to heal ourselves will only get us further lost. There isn't a correct way to heal from compulsive doing. There is an old saying which seems very appropriate here which states simply "If you meet Buddha on the road, kill him." The implication is that we must each discover our individual path to beingness and health. No one can give us *our* answers and we should immediately be distrustful of *anyone* who says they can. The best way to utilize this book is to use it's suggestions to stimulate one's own ideas and solutions realizing that we must ultimately chart our own individual course.

Finally, you will notice that this book contains a few of the "John and Jane Doe" stories you will find in other books. This type of example can set you, the reader, up with false (or at least someone else's) expectations for the healing process. While publishers like them and they may help authors sell more books, they can be misleading for the reader.

Inner compulsiveness, seemingly now a deadly nemesis, could in fact provide a catalyst for change and healing for our society and the planet. In finding the path out of our compulsive doing we can also alter the way that we deal with our environment and those around us. I do not pretend to have all the answers to this complex situation. With a certain amount of courage, however, we can begin and (as with all good healing) we will need each other on the voyage.

This is much more than a book about workaholism. It is intended as a road map for understanding and undertaking that precious and ancient journey back to a powerful state of being. It is a state of being that is available to us all in this and every moment of our lives. Let us begin together our voyage of healing.

LAND OF THE BOTTOM LINE

I couldn't bribe a wino on what I used to make
My fortune was as sure as the wind
But I was free to wonder and time was on my hands
It was mine to burn and to bend

Freedom for freedom
Call that an even scheme
Give me time to wonder and to dream
I'll take the money
They'll take the time
Down to the land of the bottom line
To the bottom line

Then there came a chance to make some steady dough
Bouncing up my alley to the door
You fill your clothes with keys and damned responsibilites
Trading the maybe for the sure

All I ever wanted was to be a kid and play
Fighting every change along the way
I don't like work, but I don't like waste
And I don't like waiting for a taste

John Gorka
from *Land of the Bottom Line*, copyright 1991

The Power of Being

Dr. Christian R. Komor

CHAPTER ONE:
DROWNING IN THE SHALLOW END

A CLOSER LOOK AT THE EFFECTS OF COMPULSIVE DOING

F or someone with tendencies to be compulsive about getting things done, today's North American society can indeed be like a pool of alcohol for an alcoholic. Everywhere there are messages that we must work harder, produce more, stop fooling around and get on with the program (whether it's corporate, exercise, or the next series of social events). The pool is getting deeper, and many are drowning. Our economy is gasping for air. National debt is in the trillions, and our personal debt (relatively speaking) is often right behind. Even the environment is taking on water. We are just now beginning to realize that the vortex created as Mother Earth heads down the drain threatens to pull us under with it. That vortex is increasing in strength each day.

Can you actually *feel* the pull? It is there in the morning when you coax your body out of bed for another day of work, errands, and doing? Can you sense the void, the rousing emptiness, when finally reaching the weekend, you spend it not relaxing but making preparations for the week to come — all the while growing older? Like many of us you may be asking "What's the point?".

The problem being addressed in this and the preceding section is the effect that doing too much can have on both individuals and on the world. We need to understand that there *is* a problem, that the consequences are stress-related illness and environmental destruction, and that the problem is *not* going to be solved by working harder.

This last point is important. While we have been gradually developing methods and technologies for reducing our workload (eg., copy machines, microwave ovens, hair dryers, telephones and fax machines, computers, etc.) we are paradoxically spending *more* hours working (Schar, 1991) and getting things done! How can this be? If more tools and techniques have been developed for saving and "managing" time, why does there seem to be less time?

This critical question leads to a powerful new way of looking at our society's problems with doing too much. It would appear that *external solutions are not enough*. New technologies and devices are not reducing the pressure in our lifestyle. It *must* be something else that is happening. That something else has to do with what happens *inside* of us regarding work and the things we do that keep us so busy. It is within our own perceptions, experience, and psychology that we must look for answers to our problems with stress and time management.

This situation is again comparable to that with alcohol and the alcoholic. When the alcoholic feels that his or her life is out of control, the solution is obvious, drink more and feel better. Are we overdoers any different? If I am feeling pressured by my job why not just buy a new cellular telephone so I can get more sales calls done in less time? What I end up doing in reality though, is throwing another work/log on the fire. Now I have to work harder to afford my new phone bill and people can call me up even when I am not in the office! Not only that, but I further *externalize* my identity. By looking for a solution *outside* of me I naturally am not looking *inside*.

This process of *externalization* is both a cause, and effect of our patterns of compulsive doing. We are, in a very real sense, caught in an endless cycle — we are indeed putting out the fire with gasoline. *Doing* is not the answer to *doing*. The answer is in the quality of our *being* — but the evidence is that we are not yet seeing the reality of the trap that we have set for ourselves. (The exercises that are presented later in this book will focus on redirecting energy inward and taking control of our situation — not by controlling the environment, but by accepting and nurturing ourselves.)

Also related to the idea of externalization is the tendency to fall into thinking that the stress around us is *inherently* stressful. A wide number of studies (Penzer, 1985; Nagy, 1985; Homer, 1985) have shown that personality has a significant impact on how we perceive the stress of the environment. Those with tendencies towards perfectionism, parsimony, goal-orientation, obsessive-compulsive behavior, and fast-pace living are likely to absorb more stress from situations that others would find neutral, or even relaxing. Workaholics are workaholics even when they are not at work just as alcoholics are alcoholics even when they are not in the bar drinking.

This leads to the inescapable conclusion that we cannot just change the environment, or "manage" our time and expect results. The voyage towards a healthier approach to the things we need to do and accomplish in life has to be an inner one. If we try to fix the situation by changing what is around us we will end up with — well, what we have ended up with!

In the first section of this book the effect that stress tends to have on our bodies was mentioned briefly. One indicator of where our fast-paced society is taking us can be seen in the type of physical problems we are having. In spite of the dramatic advances that have been made in pharmaceutical and surgical science, our North American society is being plagued with a variety of stress-related illnesses. Heart attacks, are the number-one killer for half our population and the other half (women) are quickly catching up. (Interestingly, the highest frequency of heart attacks occurs on Monday mornings — the traditional start of our workweek!)

Increasingly, contemporary research points toward dramatic mind/body links between environmental stress and various physical disorders. High blood pressure, cancer, strokes, sleep disturbances, serum cholesterol levels, gastrointestinal problems, arthritis, respiratory illnesses, diabetes, headaches, back pain, allergies, and immune system problems all are influenced by the stress of life.

Here too we are throwing more gasoline onto the fire without getting at the real problem. As a society we invest more and more time in exercise, nutrition, and dietary supplements, yet we are dropping dead of these diseases, and many others, at an alarming rate. In fact, many obsessive-compulsives who eventually develop stress-related illnesses have exhibited outstanding records of physical self-maintenance. It's almost as if compulsive doers protect the ability to *do more* by popping vitamins and working out.

The signs of wear and tear in the environment can also not be ignored. Heavy investment in productivity is using up our resources at an alarming rate. Drive by any major office building on a winter evening and you'll see the lights of toil and effort still burning late into the night, consuming precious electrical energy. Streams, rivers, and sky are groaning with the burden of consumer orientation. Industrial accidents are taking their toll, along with the day-to-day dumping of toxic wastes and by-products of manufacturing. Consumer landfills threaten to overrun our living space, yet we continue to act as a disposable culture, working harder all the while to purchase new things to replace those we throw out. The various organizations responsible for monitoring the "state of our planet" (Hollender, 1990; Brown, 1990) report that we have never been closer to wreaking permanent and life-threatening damage on the world.

In spite of all these signs that something is dangerously wrong with society's direction, we continue to work harder and attempt to accomplish more each day. It's as if we're searching for some elusive prize that someone, somewhere, told us we'd earn if we're willing to keep our nose to the grindstone and delay gratification and happiness just long enough to "make it". (Never mind that your nose is not much more than a stub by that time!)

In an age where we have a higher standard of living than any other before, when our discretionary time has supposedly increased dramatically, we are seeing more and more people suffering from stress-related disorders, anxiety, and a pervasive inability to relax. Counselors across the country are reporting that greater and greater numbers of clients are struggling with a loss of identity, purpose and self-direction. Employers who once complained of lack of initiative on the part of workers are now talking about their employees' deteriorating health and social lives as a result of overwork and exhaustion.

Both our society and each individual in our society can be viewed in reference to compulsive doing. It is not possible to live in our society and avoid having our life effected by this issue any more than a fish can live in water and not get wet!

Those who tend to be compulsive doers, however, are most likely to struggle on a personal level with doing and shoulding. We in particular are *highly* affected by society's doing addiction and have the stress-related illnesses to prove it. The task of healing is even greater because of the *context* we are living in, where an individual is so often defined not by who they *are* but by what they *do*. Obsessive-compulsive and work-addicted persons, individuals with anxiety disorders, and Type-A folks are all at special risk. This book will be particularly helpful for these persons, but also in more general ways for anyone living in our doing-addicted, compulsive society.

A Time magazine cover story (April 8, 1991) discussed the shift that is happening in American values from trendiness and materialism to homelife, basic values, and simpler pleasures. If you felt weary just reading my description of the fast-paced world around us earlier you are not alone. As a society, we are gradually beginning to grow tired of the power lunches, the trendy clothes, and the expensive foreign cars. Our focus as a nation is changing, but there is a problem! For so many years our culture has been so geared toward outward achievement and production that we have neglected to develop the *specific skills* needed to do anything else.

The North American identity is that of a nation of broad shoulders, industry, and achievement. We have become the world leaders in so many areas of production and technology that we have lost count. We are clearly a "success story" in the history of the world, *but we do not know how to be*! We are addicted to accomplishing, doing, shoulding, and forcing ourselves to achieve. Think, for instance, of the last time you tried to take time off from work. Some are better at it than others, but a common complaint today is of an inability to slow down, even when the opportunity is there to do so. It's hard to "just say no" to work.

You may have heard the popular statement that "conflict is opportunity" (Crum, 1987). This is a concept that is difficult to see when we are in the stormy waters of struggle and stress and the waves are crashing around us. Yet it is at those very times that we most need to remember this simple and profound truth. Although we may struggle with our tendencies toward compulsivity and doing, we can also find powerful potential within our struggle for growth and healing, both for ourselves and society.

On the other side of our compulsive doing is a powerful, spontaneous aliveness filled with energy and creativity. Our compulsive tendencies can paradoxically lead us to uncover the natural *power of being* that lies within like a gift waiting to be opened.

Healing from compulsive doing is not a panacea for the ailments of modern society. It is, however, a reality that our personal and social addiction to work, achievement, and accomplishing is a major contributor to many of the personal and social problems around us. This book will demonstrate how healing our compulsive doing can cause a qualitative shift in how we view not only our own self, but also our world and in how we treat us!

I don't know about you, but your author tends to get fidgety reading books that spend 9/10ths of their attention on what is wrong and 1/10th on how to recover from it. Hopefully, the above discussion combined with your own personal experience will serve to provide an outline of the *problems* we are facing. The majority of this book will address the need for specific solutions which can lift us gradually out of the mode of doing and into the world of being where we are naturally meant to be.

The next several chapters will briefly outline a description of compulsive doing, some things that make it worse, and ideas on how to heal the compulsive doing in our lives and in the world. Let us first begin with a closer look at the ways that compulsive doing as a lifestyle has affected you as an individual.

CHAPTER TWO:
CHARTING A COURSE

YOUR PERSONAL COMPULSIVE DOING CHARACTERISTICS

A s you have probably noticed in Chapter One, one of the basic ideas behind this book is that for someone living in our society it is almost impossible to remain unaffected to some degree by compulsive doing. I don't believe that it's possible to really participate in today's society and not have one's perceptions altered by the high investment we have in accomplishing, doing, shoulding, and working.

This Chapter is designed to provide you with an opportunity to look more closely at the manner and *extent* to which you personally are being affected by the issue of compulsive doing. We will also look at some of the specific *effects* of compulsive working, achieving, accomplishing, shoulding, and forcing. In

Chapter Three we will look deeper into the formation of compulsive doing, both at an individual level and in terms of society. At that point we will seek out a more precise *definition* of compulsive doing. For the purposes of this Chapter, stay aware of that sense of your own compulsive doing tendencies that led you to pick up this book in the first place. Let that inner awareness guide you and serve as your own definition as you proceed.

As a psychologist assisting people who are struggling with work addictions, compulsive and Type-A behavior, I've become aware that there are many different patterns and forms of compulsive doing behavior. For some the behavior centers primarily around the workplace. Such individuals complain that when they are at work they feel so driven and harried that, at the end of the day, they can scarcely remember what they did. Others experience a less work-specific do-aholism. For them the process of simply living in our society brings with it a sense of drivenness and compulsion to be productive that makes it difficult to slow down no matter what the situation.

There are also many *levels* of compulsive doing. For some, there is only a faint influence. Others feel continually overwhelmed by the compulsion to achieve, produce, or at least keep busy. For many of us, our doing addiction takes us by surprise. We may not realize that we are being compulsive in our approach to life until one day we look around and notice that our children are grown, life is half over, and we are not even sure what happened.

There appear to be many different types of compulsive doing, probably as many as there are compulsive doers. Three of the major types of compulsive doing are:

1.) *Acting out (Compulsive Doing)*. Those of us who are acting out our compulsive doing are over-working, over-committing and over-shoulding ourselves. We are denying and repressing our uncomfortable feelings through the *process* of being active. In this mode we are externalizing our focus out into the world through controlling and caretaking. The extent of our acting out behavior can vary greatly as illustrated below. The "classic" work addict, or Type-A person may fall into this category.

2.) *Acting in (Work anorexia)*. When we are acting in our compulsive doing we're in a state of denial. In this mode we may look like we're inactive or laid back, but we're really in a state of *resistance* toward our compulsivity. This may lead us to become non-productive, failure-prone, and inactive. Persons with little career or life direction may fall into this category.

3.) *Doing bulimia*. When we are doing "bulimic" we fluctuate between acting out our compulsive doing and denying it through lethargy and inactivity. This mode of compulsive behavior seems to be less common. (Those Sherlock Holmes fans among you will recognize the great detective as one famous work-bulimic.)

Acting out, acting in, and bulimic styles seem to be present in all sorts of compulsive behavior including: eating disorders, gambling, substance addiction, sex addiction, relationship addiction, etc. The commonality is in the desire to escape from life's pain through an unhealthy obsession with an addictive substance, or in the case of compulsive doing, the addictive process. (More on all this in Chapter Three.)

Whether we're acting in or acting out our compulsive doing, the level of compulsivity may vary from very strong to very mild or anywhere in between. Table One illustrates this theory utilizing the bell-shaped curve of normal population distribution.

TABLE ONE: Normal Population Distribution of Compulsive Doers

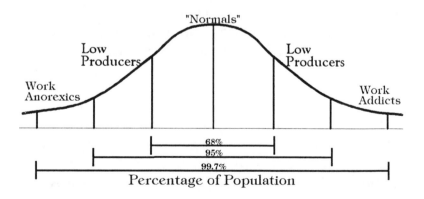

Using this curve we can see that for most people compulsive doing has only moderate impact. As family therapists have discovered, however, it's likely that only a small percentage of the population grows up in

fully functional or "normal" families. This makes it unlikely that the majority are able to negotiate society's tendencies toward excessive doing without being negatively affected to some degree. "Normal" in our society is no longer the same as "healthy."

In interpreting Table One it is important to take into account the reality that the social context is one in which compulsive doing has become accepted as part of the "ground of being". We may fall somewhere in the middle of the curve and still be far too controlled by compulsive doing in our life. Just as we are now re-norming ourselves in terms of what constitutes healthy use of such substances as tobacco and alcohol, we need to look at our norms regarding work and its addictiveness. Authors John Friel and Linda Friel (Friel and Friel, 1987) point out that often what is regarded as normal is not necessarily *healthy*. Thus, I can be in the center, or most "normal" range of Table One and still be dysfunctional in my relationship to work!

If we look at other societies, for example, we see dramatically different levels of work and productivity. While we in the U.S. produce more goods and have a higher standard of living, other societies may play more and spend more time with their families.

It is also interesting to note that people who *report* feeling relatively free of tendencies toward compulsive doing seem to fall at *either* extreme (far right or left) on Table One. What seems to be happening with persons at either extreme is that their denial system is so strong that they are unable they are acting in or out). This condition is similar to the alcoholic who refuses to acknowledge that drinking a pint of liquor each day is a sign of a drinking problem even though everyone around him/her can easily see that he/she is alcohol addicted.

In looking at our personal level of compulsive doing, it is helpful to have some criteria against which to measure ourselves. The Over Doing It Screening Test, or ODIST (pronounced "Odd-ist"!) which follows is based on my clinical experience with compulsive doers, and the types of symptoms with which they most often struggle. These are not all of the symptoms that exist. Several other writers (Robinson, 1989) provide lists of behavior for assessing "work addiction" which are also applicable to compulsive doing.

If you decide to take the ODIST it is important to keep in mind that compulsive doing is a *subjective* experience which cannot be fully captured by an objective   measurement   device   (even   one   as sophisticated as the ODIST!). The ODIST provides some guidelines to begin to get a sense for your level of compulsive doing. These are only guidelines and not a substitute for your personal experience of yourself. You may find it helpful to refer back to your personal ODIST score as you proceed through this book. It can serve as a reference to point out your particular areas of compulsive doing.

OVER DOING IT SCREENING TEST (ODIST)

NOTE: Compulsive doing affects all aspects of an individual's life (e.g., chores at home, recreation activities, social relationships, etc.). The items below are intended to be applied to your lifestyle in general and not specifically to your job or employment. For the purposes of this test the term "doing" is used interchangeably with the term "work". Both are intended to represent any form of activity, project, accomplishment or "should". Note that individuals can have normal work hours and few excessive demands at their jobs and still suffer from compulsive doing.

INSTRUCTIONS: This inventory is designed for your personal use. Take your time and answer each item truthfully. Most people find that their first response is the most accurate. For each item decide if it NEVER applies to you (0 points), SOMETIMES applies to you (1 point), or FREQUENTLY applies to you (2 points). When you have completed all 60 items add up your total score. To evaluate your score, check it against the MILD, MODERATE, and SEVERE ranges.

SCORE — NEVER (0); SOMETIMES (1); FREQUENTLY (2)

	ITEM	0	1	2
1.	I frequently find myself rushing from one task to the next.	__	__	__
2.	I find it very difficult to say "no" to requests of my time and energy.	__	__	__
3.	I often find my thoughts straying to work or projects, even during time I could be relaxing.	__	__	__
4.	I often feel that I must "caretake" others. I feel guilty if I do not do things I "should" to help people.	__	__	__
5.	It is difficult for me to "do nothing" (e.g., sit down without reading, watching television or "keeping busy").	__	__	__

6. I believe that there are many projects and tasks which require my presence and could not be completed without me. ___ ___ ___

7. It is very important to me to be in "control" of my surroundings. I get uncomfortable when I am not "on top" of things in my environment. ___ ___ ___

8. I have found that my social life has been diminished as the result of all the things I need to do. ___ ___ ___

9. I become frustrated when I am not able to complete a task which I started. ___ ___ ___

10. I frequently find myself agreeing to do things which require me to work beyond my required time limits. ___ ___ ___

11. I often find it necessary to eat my lunch at my desk or to skip lunch altogether. ___ ___ ___

12. I become irritable when my work pattern is interrupted by others. ___ ___ ___

13. My work occupies more than 40 hours per week on a consistent basis. ___ ___ ___

14. I feel angry, irritable, or resentful much of the time. ___ ___ ___

15. I often find myself doing more than one thing at a time. ___ ___ ___

16. I frequently find it difficult to concentrate because there are so many things that demand my attention. ___ ___ ___

17. I seem to get very little satisfaction or pleasure from all the things I do considering the time that I put in. ___ ___ ___

18. I don't like to "waste" time. (for example, I read if I am eating alone.) ___ ___ ___

19. Now and then I notice that I feel "numb" or disconnected from my body. ___ ___ ___

20. My enjoyment and satisfaction in my home life has been negatively affected by my need to work or keep busy. ___ ___ ___

21. Others who are close to me would say that I work too much, or that I am not available for recreation. ___ ___ ___

22. When I have time off I feel irritable, empty, or purposeless. ___ ___ ___

23. I have experienced physical problems which I believe, or have been told, are related to my level of stress (e.g., chronic headaches, backaches, high blood pressure, ulcers, strokes, heart disease, stomach problems). ___ ___ ___

24. I catch myself thinking about work or planning what I need to take care of next while others are talking. ___ ___ ___

25. I avoid having time off when I do not have something to do, or a "project". ___ ___ ___

26. I have had to make efforts to control my work hours and/or the amount of work that I take on. ___ ___ ___

27. I occasionally have caught myself "hiding" work that I want to do from others so they do not see me working. ___ ___ ___

28. I feel guilty at times about my need to work or keep busy. ___ ___ ___

29. I have had to give up relationships and/or social activities because of the demands of my work. ___ ___ ___

30. It is difficult or impossible for me to stop a task half-way through. ___ ___ ___

31. It is difficult for me to discuss a reduction in my work with others. ___ ___ ___

32. I feel that my life is often controlled by the things I "should" do rather than what I "want" to do. ___ ___ ___

33. One or both of my parents were not as available as I wished them to be because of their work commitments. ___ ___ ___

34. I fear I may become a failure if I don't work hard enough. ___ ___ ___

35. I feel that my work behavior is unmanageable or out of control.   ___ ___ ___
36. I find that my body is often tense.   ___ ___ ___
37. I tend to judge my accomplishments based on how others view me.   ___ ___ ___
38. I often have difficulty falling asleep or maintaining sleep during the night.   ___ ___ ___
39. I have one or more activity which I used to do for leisure that I now use to make money.   ___ ___ ___
40. I feel envious or irritated with people who seem comfortable relaxing.   ___ ___ ___
41. I find it difficult to relax.   ___ ___ ___
42. I am frequently late for things. Others have "given up" waiting for me.   ___ ___ ___
43. I often feel that I am less worthy or worthwhile than others in spite of my efforts and accomplishments.   ___ ___ ___
44. I frequently look to others for clues as to how I should feel or act.   ___ ___ ___
45. My daily life often seems to have a "drivenness" or obsessive quality.   ___ ___ ___
46. I frequently find myself feeling isolated from others, or lonely.   ___ ___ ___
47. I seem to find myself forgetting things more often than others around me.   ___ ___ ___
48. I often have the feeling that I need to keep everything together, or get things "all set".   ___ ___ ___
49. I have times when I am able to work non-stop yet at other times I feel it is difficult to do anything at all.   ___ ___ ___
50. In truth I am relatively indispensable in my career or job.   ___ ___ ___
51. I would describe myself as being a "perfectionist".   ___ ___ ___
52. I find myself frequently wanting to be in control of projects or relationships even when I do not need to be.   ___ ___ ___

53. I find it difficult to "open up" to others, or show my feelings and needs to them.   ___ ___ ___
54. I often find myself getting physically ill. I experience physical illnesses more frequently than others seem to.   ___ ___ ___
55. I often experience myself as "set apart" or as being "different" from others.   ___ ___ ___
56. I find myself often relying on lists in order to make sure I get everything done that I need to.   ___ ___ ___
57. I seem to be less emotional and have less feelings than others do.   ___ ___ ___
58. I frequently find myself feeling worn out or exhausted.   ___ ___ ___
59. I frequently find that I have not allowed enough time to finish a project.   ___ ___ ___
60. I take "homework" with me even during relaxation time (e.g., vacations, meal times, etc.).   ___ ___ ___

SCORING: Total the number of points in each of the three columns.   ___ ___ ___
Add all three columns together to get your
ODIST TOTAL SCORE   ___

MILD COMPULSIVE DOING   -25 TO 45 points
MODERATE COMPULSIVE DOING   -45 to 60 points
MODERATE/SEVERE DOING   -60 to 80 points
    (Addiction Level)
SEVERE COMPULSIVE DOING   -80 points & above
    (Addiction Level)
(Note: Scores higher than 81 are of increasing severity.)

One of the most useful things about the ODIST is that it can provide an opportunity to take a look at the range of behaviors and symptoms we might have that are indicative of compulsive doing. We must come to understand that compulsive doing is *not* just overworking or spending too many late nights at the office. Compulsive doing is a complex syndrome which cannot be judged by outside behavior alone.

For those familiar with the area of stress management, there are some interesting parallels of. From the items on the ODIST, it can be seen that an obvious outcome of obsessive-compulsive behavior is STRESS! Although compulsive doers who are in denial about their compulsivity sometimes report a remarkable absence of stress, those who are actively involved in the healing process know that this is a major problem. Compulsive doing and stress do go together. Not all stressed-out people are compulsive doers, but *all* compulsive doers are stressed.

Some typical symptoms of psychophysiological stress to be on the look-out for are:

Cognitive
cynicism
depersonalization
compulsivity
confusion
disorientation
distractibility
forgetfulness

Physical
accidents/carelessness
illness
headaches/backaches
lowered immune response
sleep disturbances
stomach problems

Emotional

Behavioral

helplessness	absenteeism
withdrawal	complaining
depression	blaming
irritability	agitation/lethargy
no enjoyment	frequent errors
mood swings	addictions

In looking at your own life, if you see some, or many of the above symptoms present it's likely that you are doing too much.

Another way to develop a sense for how close, or far away we are from our power of being is by looking to see if the following *positive* qualities *are* present in our life by answering "yes" or "no" to items such as:

	YES	NO
My sleep is "sweet", refreshing and satisfying.	_____	_____
My weight is normal for my age and height.	_____	_____
My life is exciting and energetic.	_____	_____
I smile and laugh frequently and naturally.	_____	_____
The world feels sensual to me.	_____	_____
I am able to relate easily with others and still maintain my personal identity and boundaries.	_____	_____
My life is characterized by lightness and spontaneity.	_____	_____

When we're tuned into our natural self, the self that knows how to *be*, we can answer "yes" to the questions above. When we are pacing ourselves and living for today, excess stress has no opportunity to build up in our life. When we are listening to ourselves and functioning from a position of choice, events and people around us do not catch us off guard or overwhelm us.

The list of symptoms on the preceding pages can be viewed as helpful warning signs that we are heading into the "compulsive doing zone". The appropriate response is to say "Thank you" to the stress symptom(s) we are experiencing and *then* begin to shift focus toward regaining the power of being. When we do so we will be able to answer "yes" to the second list of qualities above (More on this in Chapter Seven.)

It is important to note that stress is a normal part of the human condition. As stress management professionals point out, we need to have some stress in order to be productive. We also, however, need to be able to *recover* from stressful situations. It is in the absence of the ability to recover from stress in healthy ways that the compulsive doer differs from the general population. The following graphs represent the difference between a healthy stress response and that experienced by the obsessive-compulsive doer. These charts can help you develop a feeling for the effect that stress has in your life.

GRAPH I: Healthy Stress Response

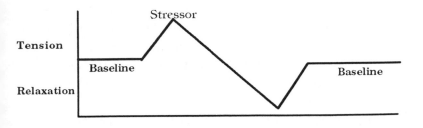

GRAPH II: Compulsive-Doing Stress Response

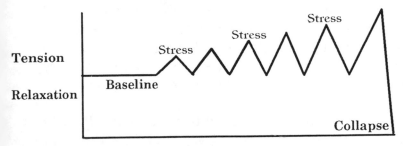

As you can see by the second graph, compulsive doers experience a gradually cumulative and additive stress-effect over time. Rather than experiencing resolution, the basic level of stress experienced by the compulsive doer gradually escalates. As the compulsive person copes with more and more activities, projects, and tasks they become acclimated to higher and higher levels of stress. Eventually, there comes a point of physical, emotional, mental, or social collapse.

Notice that Graph II bears a striking resemblance to the process of addiction to a substance or chemical. Recent research (Milkman and Sunderwirth, 1987) suggests that doing addicts may indeed develop an

occurs during stress. This may assist in accounting
for the addictive nature of compulsive doing and its
tendency to escalate over time. My clinical experience
has been that compulsive doing is very difficult to
work through. Small wonder this might be the case
if we are becoming addicted to our own body's
response to stress.

Being aware of the symptoms of stress can help in
looking for these symptoms in ourselves. We can
then use them as markers, or sign posts that we are
doing too much. When we begin noticing we're
having trouble sleeping through the night, are having
more accidents, or we're forgetting to do things we
normally would remember, it's time to take inventory
of our compulsive doing and start refocusing on *being*.

Taking inventory in regard to compulsive doing is
a very personal process. Everyone has different
symptoms and signs. Unlike substance addictions
(e.g., drugs, food, or alcohol) which can be more
objectively measured, compulsive doing is a process.
It's not as easy to measure a state of consciousness as
it is a liquid or a pill. We cannot rely fully on the
feedback received from the environment. It is far
more likely that an alcoholic will hear helpful
"feedback" from friends about excessive drinking.
Compulsive doers are most often praised by those
others for their behavior. If we buy into this it
simply reinforces the destructive process of self-
devaluing and loss of identity that compulsive doing
has at its core.

In the first two chapters we have defined some of the problems with compulsive doing and the stress that results from this process. We have also taken a closer look at the effects of compulsive doing in your personal life. In the next chapter we will seek a deeper definition of the compulsive doing process and how it works within the individual and society.

CHAPTER THREE:
MOVING INTO DEEPER WATERS

UNDERSTANDING THE PROCESS OF COMPULSIVE DOING

L et us take a closer look at the patterns and forms of compulsive doing and its developmental origins in human beings. While this is primarily a book about how to heal ourselves from compulsive doing, it is also important to understand the nature of our difficulties. The roots of compulsive doing are complex and lie both within our own lives and within society. It is an *interactive* process. Some people are *very* doing oriented and obsessive-compulsive and others are less so. Some social environments are only mildly affected by compulsive behavior and others are awash with shoulds, achievement, performance pressures, and stress. The answers lie in both directions.

In order to simplify the process of looking at and better understanding the nature of compulsive doing it will be helpful to pose several questions which people commonly ask when seeking to understand the compulsive doing process:

1.) What is compulsive doing and healthy being?

2.) How does compulsive doing become part of our lives?

3.) What is the process of compulsive doing? How does it work?

4.) What is the effect of compulsive doing on the family?

5.) How does compulsive doing develop as a cultural norm?

What is Compulsive Doing?

It is important to understand that compulsive doing, shoulding, perfectionism, workaholism, "hurry sickness", Type-A behavior, and what has traditionally been known in the world of professional psychology as Obsessive-Compulsive Personality (an anxiety disorder), are all basically the same. There are those who split hairs over this fact but the truth is that to a large degree they each overlap. Thus, when we seek to define the process of compulsive doing we need to take into account the definitions already established for these problem areas. There will be more on this later, but for now it's simply important to realize that these terms are interchangeable in defining a process of compulsive doing.

A number of authors have published material related to each of these problem areas. The most recent treatment-related literature has appeared in the area of workaholism. This is probably because addictions in general are currently enjoying a period of high media exposure. Whatever the case, these works provide important reading for defining the process of compulsive doing. The most recent are by Bryan E. Robinson (1989, 1992) and Diane Fassel (1990). Both Robinson and Fassel provide helpful criteria for defining compulsive doing via their contribution in the area of work addiction. Fassel provides descriptions of four separate types of what she terms "workaholism" and six primary characteristics of the workaholism process. Robinson outlines 20 characteristics of compulsive doing and also provides a special test (WART) for assessing the degree of compulsive working. These materials are very helpful and may provide background for a definition of compulsive doing.

Compulsive doing is defined in this book in very broad terms. In my own experiences, and in counseling work with other obsessive-compulsives, I have become convinced that workaholism, as used by Fassel and Robinson, is actually only descriptive of a part of the lifestyle that compulsive doers tend to adopt. We need to look at much more than an individual's worklife to understand the meaning of compulsive behavior. There are many obsessive-compulsives who do not work long hours. There are many workaholics who do not appear to be overachievers. I know many Type-A people who seem to take care of themselves very well through proper diet, exercise, and time management. Workaholism is simply another term for an internal process which has been known for a long time. It is an *internal* process and cannot be judged by outside standards. It is more than just work behavior that defines compulsive doers, it is our *inability to be*.

Compulsive doing has much in common with Obsessive-Compulsive Personality Disorder (OCPD) found in the Diagnostic and Statistical Manual of Mental Disorders (American Psychiatric Press, 1987). Not all compulsive doers can be labeled as obsessive-compulsive, or all Obsessive-Compulsive people as compulsive doers, but the parallels are striking (Pietropinto, 1986).

For example, one of the primary features of OCPD is engaging in repetitive behavior, images, or ideas that interfere with healthy daily functioning (Naughton, 1987). This behavior is not connected to the real demands of the situation. In compulsive doing patterns of shoulding, forcing, and compulsive accomplishing are developed that are not connected to the actual demands of the environment. Other traits that persons with OCPD have in common with compulsive doers are: exhibiting an excessive devotion to work; limited ability to express tender emotions; perfectionism that involves preoccupation with trivial details; indecisiveness; and attempts to control and caretake others. OCPD is arguably the most common psychological disorder among both clients *and* therapists today.

Compulsive doing also has much in common with what has come to be known as the Type-A personality. Type-A personality was initially identified by a group of cardiologists who wondered why the front edges of their office chairs were being worn down while those in the offices of their non-cardiology colleagues were not. These cardiologists found that *their* patients tended to perch on the edge of their seats ready to rush off to their next appointment. As they researched this phenomenon they began to discover that their patients shared common qualities of drivenness, perfectionism, competitiveness, and a high need for achievement that were not seen in the general population. Thus, the label Type-A personality was born. Most compulsive doers harbor traits of the Type-A personality.

With the above definitions in mind, compulsive doing can be defined as: *a fear-based response to living characterized by the loss of one's self-ownership and spontaneous aliveness to the act of doing, working, or achieving something external to oneself that one feels one should do or achieve. Most often the individual has a feeling that they have lost touch with what they want to do and are acting upon what they think they should do.* The compulsive doing process also assists the person in avoiding difficult feelings or experiences. Frequently these painful feelings or experiences involve rejection and abandonment, fears of either, or both. Often caretaking and controlling are the mechanisms of this obsessive-compulsive process.

Again, compulsive doing is similar to what other people call workaholism, "hurry sickness", Type-A Behavior, or perfectionism. Compulsive doing is the tendency to do what we think we *should* do instead of what we *choose* to do. Compulsive doing is a lifestyle in which the demands of the environment gradually take precedence over internal feelings, needs, and responses. In the end, compulsive shoulds take over and the ability to be spontaneous and uninhibited is lost. In a sense, life gets turned inside out so that what is external becomes more important than what is internal.

One of the best ways to define compulsive doing is in terms of the tendency to be compulsive or spontaneous in what we do. See if the activity and lifestyle we are involved in comes from a sense of choicefulness, or a sense of goal-oriented drivenness. Many have the idea that life is filled with things that need to get done. The truth is that at its essence, life is entirely optional. Ultimately, if you think about it, we don't even have to stay alive if we don't want to. Yet so many of us live as if everything we get into is a *should*. The difficult truth is that even the most valuable task or endeavor loses it's inherent worth when done without a true sense of desire and spontaneity. Even things that are supposed to be "recreational", or just for "fun" can become part of the problem. There are many stressed-out "playaholics" with piles of toys and no sense of being.

Compulsive doing is defined mainly as a *process* rather than a *substance* addiction. This is a very important distinction between two general types of addiction. Substance-oriented addictions include those to alcohol, drugs, food, shopping, or cigarettes. Process-oriented addictions include those to relationships, sex, gambling, work, etc. There is much overlap between the two general types of addiction. For example, gambling addictions can include both process (the thrill of the game) and substance (the rush of the win). (Remember, everyone has *some* addictive behavior. Addictions are simply a tool to avoid facing life head on.)

Some research (Milkman and Sunderwirth, 1987) is suggesting that compulsive doers actually struggle with both a process and substance addiction. Compulsive behavior stimulates the body to produce certain neurochemicals which then become acclimated by us. This could, in part, account for the difficulty which most compulsive doers have in establishing an ongoing healthy lifestyle.

Both process and substance addictions can be hazardous to health. One major difference is that with a substance addiction, the life-threatening object is outside of oneself and thus more identifiable. A process addiction, by its very nature, involves a less tangible, less concrete sort of substance. The substance is, to a large extent, within the individual. Compulsive doers may not even need to be actually doing or accomplishing to experience addiction. Even relaxation activities can feel compulsive and dominated by shoulds and perfectionism.

Compulsive doing has both aspects of a compulsion (feeling compelled) and an addiction (becoming habituated). Compulsive doers feel compelled to work and force and strive and give in to the shoulds of life. We then become acclimated to the level of compulsivity which we have established.

At the core of compulsive doing is the aspect of externalization of what should be internal. An obsessive-compulsive can approach going for a bike ride on a sunny day as something that must, or should be done, rather than something wanted. When "want tos" have all become "shoulds", (whether officially at work 16 hours a day, or just running around "getting things done"), the process of compulsive doing has taken over life.

What is Healthy Being?

The experience of healthy being — as contrasted with compulsive doing — will be discussed in detail in Chapter Seven. For the present, however, it is necessary to establish an operational definition to which we can refer.

It is important to understand that the power of being is within from birth and does not disappear, but rather is covered over by learned compulsivity taught by society and significant others. It is most evident, therefore, in society during the first few years of life.

Healthy being is the polar opposite of compulsive doing and (paradoxically) is re-discovered and embraced by the individual as a result of struggles with compulsive doing.

Like the experience of love, healthy being by its very nature tends to elude definition. For the purposes of this book healthy being is defined as: *An experiential way of perceiving and relating to the world characterized by a spontaneous and disinhibited acceptance and expression of self. In healthy being our expressions of self flow out of a centered sense of choiceful self-ownership rather than external ideas of who we are supposed to be and what we are supposed to accomplish.* When approaching life from the perspective of healthy being, the inherent perfection and spiritual harmony in the natural world can be experienced.

In the state of *being* a powerful feeling of aliveness and connection to our bodies is experienced. The environment seems to come alive and we may be startled by the wonderful elements of the natural world. A sense of release and letting go in our relationships is developed so that others are accepted rather than controlled, or treated as objects of dependency. A sense of destiny and an acceptance of the flow of life also is likely to be present along with an awareness of God.

Chapter Seven will outline in more detail some of the aspects of *being* we are likely to encounter. For now, let us continue with an examination of compulsive doing and how it develops.

How Does Compulsive Doing Become Part of Our Life?

Those of with tendencies to focus too much on doing and not enough on being are greatly influenced by society. We also bring our personal history into the situation. Very few people grew up in homes and schools without some degree of trauma and stress. Certain types of childhood problems set up the development of compulsive habits. There are several theories which attempt to describe that developmental process.

Most of these theories come out of the study of obsessive-compulsive behavior, Type-A behavior, and work addiction, and a number of these theories seem to be at odds with one another. For example, some of the theories of compulsive behavior suggest that it is a biological predisposition toward such behavior that is responsible. In other words, tendencies toward compulsive doing are "hard-wired" into our brains and physiology. Other theories stress the role of modeling by our parents and society as being the causative factors. Still others believe that compulsive doing is developed within the personality of the individual as a result of psychological conflicts resulting from issues with parents and family.

Black-and-white, all-or-none thinking is rarely productive. Thus, it is probably most accurate to say that *some* part of each of the current theories regarding the development of compulsive doing is correct. Let me show why this may be so.

Research (Milkman and Sunderwirth, 1987) suggests that a biological predisposition to develop certain types of addictive or compulsive behavior may exist. Researchers are suggesting that it may be possible that the children of a doing addicted, Type-A, or obsessive-compulsive person can inherit a physiological predisposition to compulsive doing just as they can toward their parents' eye color or other physical traits. It is possible that brains acclimate to lifestyle and these traits can be passed to our offspring. What may happen is that obsessive-compulsives experience chronic arousal of the sympathetic nervous system (Guyton, 1977) to which the body eventually acclimates. Over time, this alteration in physiology is interpreted as a change in DNA structure. This genetic blueprinting is then passed along to our offspring. Thus, researchers suggest, even before birth the brain may be biochemically "prewired" to develop obsessive-compulsive behavior.

Carrying a biological predisposition to compulsive doing, we then enter our family of origin (mother and father, or other parent caretakers). There certain healthy and unhealthy patterns of living are encountered which we need to respond to, or cope with. Some of these patterns present situations which are ideally suited for resolution by compulsive doing. For example, if father or mother is absent from the home most of the week because of work commitments, a child may experience feelings of abandonment and worry about their value as a person who may not be worthy to have a parent's attention. The result may begetting busy to prove worthiness of that attention. As a result of the experiences during early years, a biological predisposition toward compulsivity in doing may be augmented by our internal struggles.

Simultaneously with all this activity, parents and society may be modeling obsessive-compulsive behavior, so that this becomes an *acceptable* way of handling stressful situations within the family. Most public school programs are focused primarily on content oriented education. The *process* of learning is not as important as the memorization and recitation of facts and figures. The child is often approached as a blank slate which needs to be filled in order to function in society. Learning how to learn, question, and *experience* life is not something that is valued by a culture focused on achievement and getting ahead. Thus, in addition to the biological predisposition inherited toward compulsive doing, as well as the internal conflicts that arise from personal experiences within the family of origin, society generates role expectations which focus us even more strongly on the doing aspects of life.

In the health sciences, the interactive process described above is known as the "diathesis stress theory". The diathesis stress theory states that, when under environmental stress, people suffer impairment in the area in which they have a physiologically predetermined weakness. In this case it would be a child's inherited tendency toward compulsive doing. Among other areas of support for the diathesis stress theory, as applied here to compulsive doing, is the clinical observation that obsessive-compulsive people tend to come from family lineages where compulsive doing has characteristically been present. (This seems to be true even if the person was not actually raised by the obsessive-compulsive relatives.)

Like most addictions, compulsive doing is an outcome, a symptom, or an expression of something else. *Compulsiveness is simply the manner in which avoidance of fearful and painful events and feelings in life is expressed.* Two children in different families can grow up needing to cope with similar difficulties in their families and society. One child may develop a food addiction, the other a tendency toward compulsive doing. Both addictions are symptomatic of the way in which the child managed to survive the difficulties of the family environment.

Assuming that a child is biologically predisposed to develop compulsive doing behavior (or even in cases where there is no such predisposition), what are some of the specific family of origin situations that set up an obsessive-compulsive response?

There are several typical family situations which seem to foster obsessive-compulsive responses in children which draw away from the ability to *be*. One of the most prevalent is the family where there are strong fears of *abandonment*. Although each compulsive doer must address their unique individual issues through family of origin exploration, the issue of abandonment seems to be so prevalent among compulsive doing sufferers that it merits special attention.

Abandonment fears for adults are often labeled as fears of rejection. As a child, fear of abandonment comes from an instinctive awareness that without parents we would be unable to survive. We have not yet heard the stories about infants being raised by wolves, and instinct tell us it is more likely the wolves would rather eat us! Adults are normally able to care for *physical* needs but continue to fear interpersonal *rejection*.

Fear is the basis for all compulsive behavior.

Budding obsessive-compulsives learn to deal with abandonment fears through controlling and caretaking. This is similar to the dynamics found in most other addictive disorders such as alcoholism or codependency. It is the very efforts to control that end up hurting. For obsessive-compulsives this control is extended not just toward one specific object such as cocaine or food, but to the *process* of daily living. We seek to control *activities* (with doing being a major part) and in so doing lose ourselves to the process of controlling. We become controlled by activities, just as alcoholics become controlled by the alcohol they ingest.

This desire to control can be further stimulated by several types of parental behavior. Parents might have behaved in chaotic and inconsistent ways which were frightening and raised fears of abandonment. Children thrive on acceptance and stability. When these elements are not present in the family of origin the child will do what is needed to compensate. Many budding obsessive-compulsive children are forced to assume a "hero" or "parent-to-the-parent" role in order to cope with the inconsistency or chaos in the home. The child then begins to develop the primary characteristic of the obsessive-compulsive — an abandonment of self, or "beingness", in favor of an externalized need to *do*.

Another common abandonment situation is a sense of emotional abandonment. In these families, for one reason or another, the parents (or parent) have withdrawn from the child. Left in a painful void of parental love, the child desperately begins to search for ways to win approval and entice the parent(s) back into a loving role. The most common strategy adopted by such children is that of perfectionism. Inwardly, the child assumes that something must be wrong with them or the parent would not be abandoning them emotionally.

The natural solution for the child is self-improvement. When the sought-after parental love is not forthcoming (as it will not be since the initial withdrawal by the parent is not *about* the child's worthiness), the child responds with even more of the same behavior until all sense of natural self is destroyed. Again, the end result is a loss of "beingness" and an overabundance of "doingness".

Fears of abandonment can also lead a child to develop caretaking behaviors which later become addictive. In many families, parents have not sufficiently worked through their own fears and issues before beginning to raise their children. The child's mother may have deep fears of rejection and abandonment herself. She may act this out by trying to be a "perfect parent" to her child.

While on the surface this makes for a perfect looking family, what actually happens is that the child has to adapt to mother's insecurity. Unconsciously he or she begins to "take care of mom" by not acting up or getting angry, or in any way giving mom the suggestion that she may *not* be the "perfect parent". Once again, the result is that the child loses the sense of who he or she needs to *be* as an individual in favor of what he or she needs to *do* to avoid hurting mom and becoming abandoned.

Perfectionism can also be experienced by the child who is raised within a family which has unreal expectations. We are seeing more of this today as children are placed in accelerated educational programs by parents fearful their child will not get the "head start" they need to be "successful" in life. By watching their parent's perfectionistic attitudes toward themselves, and listening to the parents' insistence that the child perform perfectly in academics and play, these children get the clear message that who they *really* are as people is not acceptable. As a result of this perception, these children are likely to fear abandonment and cast aside their sense of who they need to *be* for themselves and begin to *do* what is expected of them. They become very "acceptable", but very *dead* inside. (This, by the way, is the family of origin pattern most commonly shared by both obsessive-compulsives and eating disordered people.)

In contrast to the pattern above, some children are raised in family systems where one or both of the parents is highly dependent and fearful. The child learns to become obsessive-compulsive in order to avoid being "swallowed up" by the parent's dependency needs. Often this path is learned by watching the dependent parent's partner, who is frequently doing addicted as a way of avoiding the dependency in the relationship with their spouse.

Doing addiction can also be taken on by a child as a substitute for another unhealthy or addictive process. Watching mom or dad's frightening bouts with lethargy and immobility when intoxicated with alcohol or drugs, the child may internally designate substance abuse as dangerous and threatening. Certainly mom or dad would be better off if they were more active rather than just sitting on the couch all day in alcoholic depression. The child instinctively gets busy, substituting work for the parental addiction which is aversive to them. Eventually the child will end up as an adult sitting on the couch unable to move because of obsessive-compulsive exhaustion. The child's sense of *beingness* is supplanted and they become a "human doing".

Children can also become obsessive-compulsive through the process of rescuing their parents. This can either be indirect as implied in some of the foregoing patterns, or direct. Parents who are simply unequipped mentally and/or emotionally for the task of raising a family abound in society. Unlike voting, driving a car or practicing a profession, parenting is something anyone can do! This includes people who should never have become parents. No parent is perfect. Experts in the field of family therapy suggest that perhaps 5 to 7 percent of parents can be described as fully "healthy". Yet parents with high levels of unresolved emotional, financial, occupational, or social problems cannot help their children to feel secure and comfortable in the world. In such an environment children naturally become hypervigilent. They realize instinctively that if they don't "get busy" and try to cope with life their very survival may be threatened. These children become adultized at far too early an age. They, too, become "human doings" to avoid an even worse fate of rejection and abandonment.

All of the above familial paths to compulsive doing have certain characteristics in common. One of the most significant of these is denial. When an addictive personality is developing as a child, we are *denying* the existence of something painful. Compulsiveness protects by wrapping us in a blanket of denial. Under this blanket, feel the pain of parents' abuse, neglect, or abandonment is avoided. Later, of course, as adults we begin to suffer the side effects of this denial in failed relationships, stress-related health problems, depression, and addiction.

As our childhood denial system increases in strength we also begin to observe certain rules of dysfunctional family behavior. Among these are the rules: "Don't talk", "Don't think", and "Don't feel". Rather than protecting the child against pain, as is the case with denial, these rules tend to protect the parents against having to confront the dysfunction in

the family system. Among other things, these
dysfunctional rules create a cycle of shame in the life
of a child. The child (and later the adult) feels that
something must be deeply wrong with him or her
since no one else in the family seems to be talking
about, thinking about, or feeling the uncomfortable
things that they experience. The child becomes, in a
very real sense, a hostage to their parents'
dysfunctional patterns of living and *then* comes to
adopt them as their own. The denial system is
complete when the child does not realize that the
dysfunctional patterns came from *outside* of them and
begins believing that *they* created the problems.

The patterns presented here are several of the
more common ones found in the original families of
obsessive-compulsives. They are certainly not all of
the patterns that exist. They may also function in
combination with one another. Compulsive doers
need to return to the family of origin and look at the
issues dealt with as children. For each of us this
work will be highly individualized and personal. Like
snowflakes, no two compulsive doers fit the same
profile. What we do have in common is the *outcome*
of the combination of our physiological and emotional
backgrounds. That outcome is compulsive doing.

What is the Process of Compulsive Doing?

As is the case with all addictions, compulsive
doing is a symptom, an expression of something much
larger underneath. Beneath obsessive-compulsive
behavior is all the denied pain of childhood that we
believe we created. Through one or all of the

processes described in the previous section, we have selected compulsive doing as a way of coping with that pain. Compulsion for doing can be seen as the tip of the iceberg, beneath which are a whole raft of *fears*. The good news is that deep underneath that ice is the true self, the us that we were meant to be before the damage done in the dysfunctional formative years. Waiting there is a "child within" (Bradshaw, 1987) still full of love, aliveness and natural energy. As that inner child is rediscovered through retrospective family of origin therapy, as well as internal and external lifestyle changes, we become *ourselves* again. We recover the power to *be*.

Compulsive doing is partly control and caretaking of the environment and others in order to soothe anxieties about our value as a person and fears of rejection. In one survey of work addicted people, 30 percent of the sample group reported "inferiority feelings and fear of failure". Another 27 percent reported their workaholic type behavior as a "compulsive defense against strong anxiety"; 18 percent reported elevated "needs for approval", and 16 percent cited "fears of personal intimacy" as the driving force behind their compulsive doing (Pietropinto, 1986). All of these struggles arise out of abandonment and rejection fears at the core of the individual.

Compulsive doers are masters at these styles of relating to the world. While not all caretakers are Compulsive doers, *all* compulsive doers are caretakers and controllers of the environment. *This* is our primary style of relating to the world. Caretaking and controlling behaviors are so much a part of us, so intertwined with our identity that we may not even be aware of them. Years into recovery we may still be discovering new levels of letting go in our caretaking.

As we interact with the environment, through caretaking and controlling behavior, the sense of self-identity and self-ownership is lost. For many compulsive doers there is tremendous pain around this issue when beginning to see how non-existent we have really been. This may account for the 67 percent of workaholics who report a greater tendency to abuse alcohol than the general population (Peitropinto, 1986).

As our natural selves are rediscovered, the emptiness of relationships and activities becomes clear. *Grief* is the natural response to this loss. Many will spend a great deal of time crying during the first parts of the journey to being. This is often difficult at first for the many obsessive-compulsives who are men. Society has burdened men with an extra layer of denial which has to be worked through (Bly, 1991). For most men there is a strong prohibition against showing pain, hurt or tears. Men are allowed to get angry, but that is often where the societal permission ends. In recovery, men need to gradually coax themselves into the open and allow tears to flow when necessary.

In caretaking and controlling, there is the tendency to give away, in an unhealthy way, to others and to the environment. Doing addicts often report feelings of resentment about this with little recognition of the ability to *give* themselves permission to be off the hook. heros and caretakers are willing to do all sorts of favors for people, never letting anyone down and feeling profoundly guilty if that happens. Controllers get *everything* accomplished on time and never disappoint. Even when close to total bed-ridden exhaustion, we still finish those last few details on the project and then stay up late to get the laundry done.

It is very important to see the connection between caretaking, controlling, and compulsive doing. This is especially true as the healing process is approached. Normally obsessive-compulsive acting out is let go of first, then we become aware of the caretaking-controlling patterns toward others and the environment. We then begin to get past shame and explore the roles and patterns from childhood that are at the core of compulsive doing.

Thus, compulsive doing is a process of losing identity and a sense of natural feelings, needs, impulses and desires. Instead, the focus is external on caretaking others and controlling the environment. This is done to avoid painful fears of rejection and of not being good enough. The more this is done, the emptier it feels, and the more obsessive-compulsive behavior is used to try to resolve the situation.

What is the Effect of Compulsive Doing on the Family?

The caretaking and controlling behavior so integral to the compulsive doing lifestyle creates an unhealthy process in the family system as well. In a survey of 400 obsessive-compulsive physicians, Pietropinto (1986) found that while 49 percent of the doctors surveyed reported "higher than normal expectations for marital satisfaction", and a full 88 percent of the obsessive-compulsives in the survey were "more demanding of achievement in their children", 49 percent were likely to use "leisure" time for more work rather than pursuing family harmony. Add to this the fact that 47 percent of obsessive-compulsives choose mates who have "dissimilar personalities" and a situation exists for family struggle and conflict.

Pietropinto found that 72 percent of his sample group engaged in less frequent sexual relations than the control group. Forty fire percent reported their style of managing marital conflict as "avoidance of confrontation", a coping style not likely to breed relationship contentment.

The above survey data suggests that obsessive doers have fewer relationship skills than their peers, yet far greater expectations of marital and parenting happiness. Small wonder that 74 percent of the *spouses* of compulsive doers were found to be more likely to have sexual affairs outside the marriage. With a demanding and controlling compulsive doer in the house, spousal satisfaction is unlikely.

What seems to be particularly difficult for compulsive doers with families, is to avoid the tendency toward codependency. Codependency has come to be defined as a compulsion to "let someone else's behavior affect him or her" and a corresponding "obsession with controlling other people's behavior" (Beattie, 1987). Compulsive doers tend to get "stuck" in blaming, controlling, or trying to change their spouse's behavior rather than addressing their own issues. Often they will change mates in order to "cure" their unhappiness, only to find themselves continuing the same pattern of behavior in the new relationship.

Compulsive doers tend to regard their families as extensions of themselves. The tendency is to marry mates who value material goods and career success and who enjoy the fruits of the obsessive-compulsives labor — at least initially. Over time a great deal of frustration and resentment builds as the spouse of the compulsive doer chaffs under their overly controlling and rigid caretaking behaviors combined with long hours devoted to work or other activities.

Since compulsive doers often do not feel comfortable expressing feelings, and tend instead to caretake the spouse's feelings, unvented anger frequently brews below the surface of the marriage. Substance abuse is one likely result. Children become rebellious and angry as a result of requests for perfect academic performance, with limited offerings of praise, nurturing and affection. Children in the compulsive family learn to deny their feelings in favor of intellectualization. Humor and spontaneity are seldom modeled for children, resulting in a serious grimness in the entire family unit.

Spouses of compulsive doers also tend to have difficulty owning and expressing their own needs. They feel a certain, not so healthy safety living with a compulsive doer whose "needs" are frequently strong and demanding. Ultimately, however, this situation results in more abandonment feelings and corresponding unhappiness.

Mealtimes are probably the best example of the effect of compulsive doing on the family. Instead of spending quality time relating and sharing feelings, compulsive families often do not even sit down at the table. This hurried approach to meals leads again to abandonment fears on the part of both children and parents.

How Does Compulsive Doing Develop as a Cultural Norm?

On the surface, it's somewhat easier to define how compulsive doing becomes a part of culture than how it invades the life of the individual. It is important to do so, however, since culture has a cyclical impact on the nature and quality of families within that culture. Thus, in world cultures where the "puritan work ethic" is not as strong, less people struggling with compulsive doing as way of life are seen.

Our culture has been very successful in material terms. In spite of its ups and downs, the economic system has been remarkable for its stability and power. One of the pillars on which a capitalistic economy is based is the diligence and industry of the workers. Labor is the "backbone" of the system of production to which we have all become acclimated. Without the drive to produce, the gross national product would obviously shrivel. There has, however, been a price for this success. In fact, the indication is that a point of overload and diminishing returns has been reached. As discussed earlier, most of the physical and emotional illnesses experienced by U.S. citizens today can be traced in some degree to what is called "stress" (Komor, 1982).

Stress has been a part of our culture for so long that there are a wide variety of stress management programs, workshops, and activities. These external approaches to stress, however, do not address the internal impact which the work ethic has had on the structure of the family and the psyche of the individual. For example, males in our society are just beginning to address their grief over the *absence* of fathers during their formative years (Osherson, 1986). Generations have literally been raised by mothers while fathers were off at *work*. Fathers themselves frequently complain that they are unable to find time to spend with their offspring and that when they do they feel awkward and distant. This is just one of the ways that the work ethic has impacted our families. (Given the suffering related to the above dynamic it is not surprising that men seem to be falling prey to compulsive doing more frequently than women even when they are in comparable work situations.)

A *vicious circle* has formed between the social demands that foster compulsive doing behavior in the family and the children who go forth from those families to produce more compulsive doing in the culture.

The interactional effect between the individual obsessive-compulsive and the doing addicted society becomes self-perpetuating. The extent and frequency of compulsive doing becomes greater and greater as we move along, until eventually our bodies begin to reach their physical limits. Even the resulting health problems can, if not addressed in a healthy manner, simply lead to more obsessive-compulsive behavior in order to deal with the health problems themselves.

In Chapter Four, we will look at some of the ways in which we get ourselves hooked into compulsive doing. We will also look at a blueprint of what *not* to do, if we are truly intent on finding a healthy sense of *being* in our life.

CHAPTER FOUR:
LOOKING OUT FOR THE
ROCKS

SOME WAYS WE CAN
GET OURSELVES LOST
IN COMPULSIVE DOING

T hus far we have taken a look at the problem of compulsive doing, its effect at the personal, social, and family levels, what effects do-aholism, and how it develops in the life of the individual and society. Before proceeding to a discussion of specific strategies for healing the tendency to overwork, it will be helpful to briefly look at what *not* to do.

Unfortunately, this was the easiest chapter of this book to write. At one time or another your author has made *all* of these mistakes, most of them more often than I care to remember. Of course, the only true mistake is one that is not learned from. In the individual healing process we are likely to hit all kinds of bumps and snags. Like in a good video game these traps and triggers get progressively more diffficult and challenging as we move along. It is what is learned from these skinned knees and bruised elbows that is most important. In order to heal from compulsive doing we first have to understand what is happening and what "triggers" compulsive behavior. This chapter is designed to assist in accomplishing that.

One thing that should be strongly emphasized is that we do *not* need to, or deserve to, beat ourselves up about difficulties and slips in the area of compulsive doing. Compulsive doing becomes a part of our lives as a result of the experiences encountered as children, in society, and (probably) our physiological makeup. In addition, the world treats compulsive doing as a *positive* trait. We are encouraged and rewarded for being work addicted and suppressing feelings and needs in service of greater productivity. (With all of these factors, it is a wonder that we aren't *all* collapsed in a heap on the floor!)

Compulsiveness is one way that was learned to cope with the circumstances that were encountered in our lives. Most of us have not known any other way. This coping has served well in some areas. Most over-doers and Type-A folks tend to be outwardly successful and good providers for their family and community. The trouble is that this success is based on a *denial of self* that is painful and ultimately unfulfilling. To heal from compulsive doing and find that sense of self-ownership and fulfillment, we need to let go of shame. Shaming ourselves further about the situation and viewing ourself as defective only makes the situation worse. Compulsive doing is a process based on shame and low self-esteem and it thrives on it. *The power of being arises through acceptance of who we are and who we are not.*

Another important aspect to take note of is that it is not possible to abstain from doine. While someone who is addicted to alcohol can refuse to "touch another drop", or a television addict can have the cable disconnected, we cannot just stop *doing* things in life. This is *not* a book about never getting anything done, or being unproductive and shiftless. Rather, it is about finding balance, quality, and a sense of centeredness in life.

Towards that end, we can learn to abstain from that portion of doing that is compulsive and unhealthy and act in ways that are consistent with inner rhythms and needs. Through various methods of healing, we can learn to balance doing and being so that they eventually become one and the same. All this can be tricky, though. Even if very well off financially, the compulsive activities engaged in are not usually confined to work activities. A good do-aholic can be compulsive about *any* activity, including those that are supposed to be recreational or fun. Being and doing are not just limited to specific behaviors, but rather are best defined as *states of mind.*

With this awareness, the compulsive doer must *plan* for crises. We cannot totally avoid all the internal and external triggers. We *will* get drawn into compulsive doing, recover, and then get drawn in again. The critical element is maintaining *balance*. In order to do that we need a clear sense not only for what our triggers are but also for our own stress management balance. We need to be clearly aware of our symptoms and the triggers in the environment which get us into the compulsion to do too much. The following self-test, *The Lifestyle Monitor*, is an instrument which can be used to assess personal triggers or hooks, and their level of impact on a day-to-day basis. (*The Lifestyle Monitor* owes much of its theoretical development to the earlier work of Dr. Patrick Carnes [1989].)

THE LIFESTYLE MONITOR

The Lifestyle Monitor is designed to assist in looking at areas of life that are in balance and thus nurturing. It is also to assist in looking at areas of life that are out of balance and therefore not nurturing. For each lifestyle area that is indicated, write out four examples. First, write out two ways which indicate when the particular area that you are assessing is getting "out of whack". (For example, under the area of nutrition when my life is getting out of whack, I have difficulty in deciding how much food is healthy each day. I would therefore write "Too much/too little food" in the left hand column under the "Nutrition" category.

In the right hand column write down what, for you, is the healthy *opposite* of the unhealthy behavior just recorded. (In the above example you might record "Eating as much as my body tells me I need.") Thus, for each category create two examples of your healthy behavior and two examples of your unhealthy, or stress-induced, behavior. When finished, follow the scoring instructions at the end of The Lifestyle Monitor.

1.) ATTITUDE: Most of us develop a sense for when our personal perspective is in balance and when it is not. In looking back at those times when you were least healthy, what types of thoughts were you having? Were you defensive, resistant, locked into a fight/flight conflict, etc.? On the left, write out two examples of attitudes that indicate that your lifestyle is out of whack and (on the right) two examples of when your attitudes are "in whack".

_____   _____

_____   _____

1....2....3....4....5....6....7

2.) SLEEP: Sleep patterns are one of the first things affected when our life is in trouble. We may have nightmares. We may sleep too much, or too little. We may not be able to sleep at all because our compulsive doing has gotten out of control. What are the particular sleep disturbances you experience? How do you know when your sleep is rewarding and healthy? List your typical sleep problems and then their opposites on the right.

_____   _____

_____   _____
1....2....3....4....5....6....7

3.) SUPPORT SYSTEMS: How are your relationships affected when you are not taking care of yourself? Where does the stress show? Are you snappish at work with office staff? Do you rage at other drivers on the road? Do you become distant and withdrawn from your spouse? Give two examples of ways that your relationships are upset when you are stressed out and their opposites.

_____   _____

_____   _____
1....2....3....4....5....6....7

4.) EXERCISE AND PHYSICAL HEALTH: What do you do to take care of your physical body on a regular basis? Aerobics, meditation, running, yoga? What happens to these self-care behaviors when push comes to shove and you are feeling under pressure? Write down two and their opposites.

_____   _____

_____   _____
1....2....3....4....5....6....7

5.) NUTRITION: Ever notice how your diet can fall by the way-side when short of time and patience? Ever notice how fast food, or no food can replace good food when you are harried and hurried? What are two ways that your dietary lifestyle changes when you are under the gun? What are the opposites of these changes?

_____   _____

_____   _____

1....2....3....4....5....6....7

6.   TIME MANAGEMENT: This is often one of the areas to show the most dramatic change when compulsive doing is becoming unmanageable.   Our smooth pace becomes a wild frenzy as we dance as fast as we can to keep up with the demands we feel around us. List two primary ways that your time becomes unmanaged during stressful situations. List the healthy opposites as well.

_____   _____

_____   _____

1....2....3....4....5....6....7

7.) ENVIRONMENTAL: Are your normally fastidious ways likely to turn to slovenly sludge under pressure? Do you usually excel at taking care of chores around the house except when you are feeling stressed? Are you normally comfortably relaxed about your home duties until you're feeling in a pinch, whereupon you get manic about every little dust crumb? Write down two ways (and their opposites) you can tell when your stress level has disturbed your environmental serenity.

_____   _____

_____   _____

1....2....3....4....5....6....7

8.) RECREATION: What things do you normally do for pleasure and relaxation? What happens to these things in times of stress and strain? List two things that indicate your R&R behavior is out of whack and two opposites.

_____   _____

_____   _____

1....2....3....4....5....6....7

9.) FINANCES: How do you handle and distribute your financial resources when you are feeling at peace with yourself? Does this change when you are not so placid and serene? What have you noticed about your financial life when you are getting into trouble stress-wise? List two examples and their opposites.

_____   _____

_____   _____

1....2....3....4....5....6....7

10.)   WORK LIFE: During times of stress does your desk get piled with unopened mail? Do phone calls torment you? Does your creativity and enjoyment go down the tube? List two "bad" signs and two opposite "good" signs.

_____   _____

_____   _____

1....2....3....4....5....6....7

11.)   PERSONAL AND SPIRITUAL GROWTH: Often we tend to put work first and "personal" development last. Have you noticed the particular aspects of life that you find fulfilling, such as church, reading, meditation, or attending a support group meeting suffer as a result of stress? What happens to these activities when your life is particularly chaotic? What do things look like when you are "in balance"?

_____   _____

_____   _____

1....2....3....4....5....6....7

While there may be other lifestyle areas that are affected by your internal balance, the ones above will give a good basic overview of where you are at any particular time. Once you have written down your 44 examples (22 positive and 22 negative) pick the *one* for each category that seems most significant and put a star next to it.

Locate the line at the bottom of each category which has numbers from 1 to 7. Let 1 represent the negative example or "anchor" and 7 the positive example or "anchor". Numbers 2 - 6 are then the "shades of grey" between these two polar "anchors". Using a pencil, circle where you are at the present time between the negative and positive behavioral anchors.

Make a copy of the Lifestyle Monitor. At the end of each week rate yourself again on each of the 11 categories chosen. Notice how life stress increases proportionate to your level of compulsive doing. Also notice growth as you continue to work towards the power of being. You may begin to notice more and more 7s and less and less 1s. If so, pat yourself on the back. If not, pat yourself on the back anyway and re-dedicate yourself to taking care of your most important resource — *YOU!*

The Lifestyle Monitor is one tool compulsive doers can use to keep track of whether they are getting into the deep end in life.   As a measurement device, however, the Monitor cannot tell the most important information about your level of compulsive doing — how you *feel*. Compulsive doers are very quick to forget to check in with themselves on a continual basis to reassess the doing/being balance. It isn't at all uncommon for doing-addictive people to describe a gradual process of drifting further and further into accomplishing, caretaking, achieving, and getting things done without even realizing it. (Even reading this book can take on an obsessive quality by a true do-aholic with a high ODIST test score. "Just a few more pages and I will have read enough for tonight!")

Compulsive doers continually need to reorient themselves to how they *feel* right now. We develop a special skill at ignoring warning signals and feedback from our inner self and then pay the price later. Re-tuning the ability to listen to feeling-feedback is essential in the recovery process from obsessive-compulsive doing.

Specific "Triggers" for Compulsive Doers

Each compulsive doer is likely to have a number of "triggers" that start the compulsive cycle. It is very important to identify what these are. Get out some paper right now and list your personal triggers. Triggers are situations, people, inner experiences, external stressors, etc., that seem to occur just prior to, or in conjunction with, a build-up of compulsive doing behavior.   Most often they are things that revive old messages (see Chapter Three) from our family of origin that are painful or frightening, and make us want to run away from ourselves.

Some of the common triggers for compulsive doers include:

— Conflict in relationships
— Heavy work demands
— Sexual problems

— Embarrassing situations
— Any "rejection" situation
— Scheduling conflicts
— Being at home

— Home repair

— Being overweight
— Guilt-provoking situations
— Grief and loss

— Weekends and vacations
— Light work demands
— Change in job/residence, etc.
— Uncertain situations
— Times of financial stress
— Codependent relationships
— Being away from home
— Having and raising children
— Deadlines
— Getting married

— Getting divorced...

... or almost any situation which involves change, questions of self-worth and self-identity, or increased levels of life stress.

Weekends are one event that triggers many compulsive doers. During the week our projects and tasks keep us tuned into doing and tuned out of our fears and feelings. On weekends we may be confronted with more potential for *not* doing much of anything. That can be frightening for a compulsive doer! Where others look forward to time off work, compulsive doers find themselves in the midst of feelings that are unfamiliar. Conflicts around intimacy come to the forefront during time at home with the family. Children may be reminders of old angers toward our parents that are still lurking in the unconscious.

Once we have discovered one of our specific triggers, we may find that there are certain interventions that will help to re-balance ourselves during these times. On weekends, for example, It may be helpful to work on setting specific boundaries around needs for alone time, away from the family during the weekend. We may also balance the work-week schedule with more family time and thus take some of the pressure off the weekends. We may want to do some family of origin work around our anger if abandoned by our parents so that we can relate to our children in a healthier way.

Weekends are just one of the many situations that can trigger compulsive doing behavior. Having completed a personal list of compulsive doing triggers, study it over closely and identify any common threads running through the list. Are you compulsive about your activities at times when you are angry but don't feel comfortable expressing the anger? Is one of your triggers a certain type of person or relationship? Do you get more hooked during certain times of the day, such as the early morning? If you look closely enough at each situation you may find a similar *feeling* that you are avoiding, or with which you are uncomfortable. This gives important areas to work with in understanding what makes you tick.

What to Do in a Crisis

We can get *so* deeply into compulsive doing that we reach a state of *emergency*. In terms of looking out for the rocks in the river of compulsive doing, it is also important to be able to tell when we have actually *run aground*. Surprisingly, many compulsive doers remain in denial about compulsive doing even as they are crashing into "the wall". This wall can represent physical or emotional collapse, financial unmanageability, loss of friends, family, or job, or any of a variety of compulsive doing produced disasters. Usually this compulsive doing crisis state can be identified by the presence of a number of the cognitive, social, emotional, and behavioral traits listed in Chapter Two.

During such a crisis the individual appears to be in a frenzy of activity with no end in sight. A sense of hopelessness, desperation, emptiness, self-abandonment, and shame pervades every waking moment. Everything in the environment is viewed as a task. There is no satisfaction, only more and more to accomplish. At this stage we tend to conceal from others the out of control nature of the situation. There is danger of losing a job and/or family *because* of the very compulsive doing behaviors developed for protection. Too much control over life has led to a life that is out of control.

The compulsive doing crisis should be viewed as an *emergency*, both by the compulsive doer and those who care for them. The situation can be life threatening and it's time to get outside help. There are two things that the compulsive doer can do at this point:

1.) Immediately *slow down*. Call in sick at work if necessary. Sit on the couch, bed, or chair. Resolve not to *do* anything worklike for *at least* a week or two (See Chapter Six, "Do Nothing"). Then find a support meeting or contact a trustworthy therapist, or both. Begin to formulate a plan for recovery.

2.) Contact an inpatient recovery center that deals with compulsive doing. Make immediate arrangements to enter the program at the earliest opportunity.

3.) Remember that others have been through this before. It *will* be okay. This *could* be the awakening of a whole new way of living. What now feels like a terrible experience could be a wonderful opportunity if used properly.

Sometimes the best thing to do is to embrace the crisis being experienced. After all, most compulsive doing crises arise from the tendency to drive and force ourselves to do more and more to prove our worth, and, or avoid uncomfortable perfectionistic self-denial. The best thing to do is say "This is a total disaster and I feel awful right now." In that paradoxical moment the healing journey into our own humanity and away from compulsive doing will begin.

Remember, compulsive doing is a *process* and does not involve a substance that others can *see* us abusing. It is also condoned and even supported by culture. Admitting a compulsive doing crisis, as described above, is VERY hard to do. There is the fear that others will simply laugh, or dismiss the idea. There is the fear that we are being a "baby" or are "weak". We are used to being the "hero" that holds everything together and perseveres even when others cannot. Everything inside tells that we must *not* admit to be having a problem, especially when the problem is out of control. We need to be brave enough to listen to our inner voice in spite of all these factors. That voice is calling you to begin your journey to being. The best thing to do is say "Yes" to the call.

Knowing where the rocks are is a critical part of healthy living. It doesn't make any sense at all to keep bashing against them when they can be used creatively for growth towards being. This is especially true in the next chapter which looks at the process of family of origin exploration. Family of origin work, as described in the next chapter, is often difficult, emotionally draining, and challenging. We need all of our strength and resources to do this work. We do not want to be running around crashing into "rocks" at the same time.

Let us proceed to look at the process of recovery through family of origin exploration (or "Pumping Out the Bilges"). Retrospective personal exploration helps to find and heal the reasons *why* we tend to get into obsessive compulsive behavior in the first place.

CHAPTER FIVE:
PUMPING OUT THE BILGES

HEALING THE EARLY HURTS THAT LEAD TO COMPULSIVE DOING

C hapters Two and Three looked at how compulsive doing develops as an interaction between physiology, the family system within which we were raised, and society. We looked at several different family patterns which, alone or together, set a child up to develop a compulsive lifestyle.

This Chapter shifts the focus to look at the components of the healing process for compulsive doing. (We are getting to the really fun stuff!) The great part — maybe not exactly "great" — about having something to struggle with is that you do get a chance to get better. In the case of compulsive doing, "better" can be more than just better, it can be *wonderful!* Through efforts at self-healing we can rediscover the *power of being!*

Conflict *is* opportunity *if* approached properly. Recovering compulsive doers that have gone before can be heard to make curious statements such as: "My struggles with working too much were the best experience that ever happened to me", or "If it wasn't for my compulsive doing I never would have found what it means to really live!" The next several chapters are about the journey from the pain of compulsive doing to the exhilaration of healthy being.

Like most psychological healing processes, recovery from compulsive doing can be divided into three general phases: feelings and our developmental history; changing internal perspectives; and changing external behaviors. Each of these three approaches builds off of and complements one another.

At the base of all healing lies the experiences we went through in our family of origin. "Family of origin" therapy is a relatively new label for a relatively old process. Family of origin therapy is what many psychologists and psychiatrists have been conducting behind the closed doors of their offices for most of this century. Beginning with Freud and his contemporaries, therapists and counselors have been assisting people in unraveling the secrets of their childhood experiences. While eastern cultures have focused their healing efforts on internal perspective changes in the *present*, one great contribution of western psychology has been in identifying *familial origins* of human suffering.

During the 1980's a grass roots movement emerging from the field of alcoholism recovery has generated renewed interest in the power and possibilities of retrospective family of origin exploration. In their attempts to assist persons healing from various types of addictive and compulsive behavior, recovery counselors have begun a wide variety of programs and services that were previously unavailable. Although frequently disconnected from supportive research data, pioneering recovery counselors have acted on existing psychological healing practices and have developed a range of innovative new techniques. Many of these techniques are designed to assist in working through family of origin issues.

Family of origin work can be conducted either individually, in groups, or even in the context of actual family of origin. Unfortunately, often by the time it's realized that something is wrong and that compulsive doing has gotten unmanageable, the family of origin has drifted apart and one (or both) parents has passed away. This does not mean, however, that we will be "stuck" with the past as it was. Through family of origin exploration we can, at least on an emotional level, "rewrite" the choices made based on our past experiences.

The way in which this is done is *through our feelings*. In direct contrast to the compulsion to do too much (which is designed to help to *avoid* feelings) family of origin therapy encourages and guides in uncovering and discovering first the existence of feelings and then where these feelings came from (encounters with parents, siblings, peers, etc.). The family of origin healing process has been described in detail by a number of writers. The process itself is as complicated and unique as the individual who is participating in it.

As we begin to uncover feelings and understand where we got them from, we are also able to make connections back to our adult lives. We begin to see how these ancient fears, angers and hurts have directed our existence. We learn how choices and perceptions have been influenced dramatically by these buried feelings until there is little resemblance to our *natural* reactions, preferences and beingness. Gradually we are then free to release these patterns and *re-decide* how to interact with life and with others.

Everyone has personal issues which have led to developing compulsive doing. These issues arise from decisions made internally during childhood based on real or imagined fears. In family of origin therapy we slowly uncover these issues and bring them to light. Some possible issued/decisions related to compulsive doing are listed below:

"I am only valuable when I am busy or at work."

"I am not really acceptable to others."

"I can only do it if I can do it perfectly."

"Needing things from others means I am weak."

"Taking care of myself is selfish."

"I do not have the right to exist."

"I must be how I should be and not how I want to be."

"I am responsible for other's feelings when they are around me."

It may be helpful to look at what a typical process is like as we uncover family of origin issues.

First of all, it is helpful to seek out a qualified therapist or program that offers family-of-origin type growth experiences. There are many places to begin the search including local substance abuse treatment centers, psychologists, college or university counseling centers, or community mental health centers.

There are many types of counselors and many types of therapy. The following ingredients seem to make for a helpful counselor for compulsive doers: 1.) The therapist has worked through some of their own issues and is comfortable with *feelings*; 2.) They are not in active denial regarding addictions and doing addiction in particular; 3.) The therapist is comfortable using "active" methods of therapy such as psychodrama, Gestalt, bioenergetics and family systems role-playing; 4.) The therapist is willing to respect *your* pacing and direction. He or she assists you in finding *your* path and uncovering *your* feelings, not forcing you to fit a pre-prescribed mold for change.

Like everyone, therapists are not perfect, but your therapist needs to be comfortable with his or her own feelings and issues in order to assist you with yours. No matter what their training or educational background, a therapist who is refusing to acknowledge their own family of origin issues will tend to be blind to those of others.

Penzer (1984) points out that many therapists are themselves compulsive overdoers. Because of the caretaking and hero role issues that compulsive doers often carry into their professions, it is particularly difficult for obsessive-compulsive type therapists to deal with their personal issues in this area. For a therapist to admit to compulsive doing and the issues which underlie the addiction leads to a direct confrontation with shame that is difficult for the therapist to surmount. (Trust me on this one!) Penzer also suggests there is a link between professional insecurities and psychotherapists' dysfunctional behaviors. In short, it is wise to interview several therapists before making a selection.

Much family of origin work is done in groups. There seems to be a special power that therapy and self-help groups have that cannot be obtained through individual means. One of the most helpful and inexpensive family-of-origin type group situations that compulsive doers can participate in is Workaholics Anonymous (WA) or Adult Children of Alcoholics (ACA, or ACOA). These groups are usually open to *anyone* who comes from a dysfunctional family background (even if alcohol was not an overt issue). WA, ACA and ACOA groups can often be found meeting at Alcoholics Anonymous clubs and churches. All you have to do is find out the time and attend. Once at the meeting ask the chairperson about family of origin therapists and groups in the area. It's likely that they will be able to give some helpful suggestions.

You may also decide to get into a specialized program, or attend a workshop as you begin in the family of origin healing process. Several of the sources in the References section of this book provide information on different programs. In particular, Melody Beattie (1990) provides a wonderful compilation of the various groups and programs available around the U.S. Such programs are especially helpful for those who have begun to collapse under the weight of compulsive doing behaviors. Although most of us HATE to ask for help (especially when most needed) it's critical to do so.

Once involved in the family of origin experience selected for yourself, two things will begin to happen. You will have an opportunity to *express* feelings regarding what happened as you were growing up. You will also begin to *experience* some of those childhood feelings and patterns *within* the group itself. This is the phenomenon therapists call "transference", or the transferring of feelings toward or about your parents and significant others in your past to those around you now — in this case other group members and/or your therapist.

In both of the above ways there will be the opportunity to uncover and work through feelings and patterns which have been underlying compulsive doing. In place of acting out fears, angers and hurts, or projecting them and controlling others, you are encouraged by the therapist to feel them and take responsibility for them. Eventually, you will be able to let go of the unhealthy patterns from the past, and for-*give* them back where they originated from — to your family of origin. As you do so you begin to live more fully in the present and to be able to distinguish between old issues and feelings and the reality of present circumstances.

It is helpful to be aware that when living out of compulsive doing, we will naturally tend to *project* difficulties and fears onto those around us. If you are in a situation where you believe that those around you, or your circumstances, are *preventing* you from healing, give yourself some time to test out the validity of this notion. Even when we are *certain* that it is the other person who is *making* us feel this way, it is almost always really us at work projecting onto the other person. At the very least we *are* always free to choose as adults how and who to relate to. It is so difficult to remember this, but essential if we are going to learn to let go of control and develop the ability to accept life and those living around us.

It is important to note that this process is not about blaming our parents for the treatment received as a child. Rather the goal is to *detach* from the past. Children tend to swallow whole significant other's views and treatment. As we heal we are increasingly able to say "That's not me. I don't have to be that way or view life through those old perspectives. I give those feelings and beliefs back to the person I learned them from!"

As we begin to realize that *we* are not the negative *patterns* picked up along the way, we become free to re-choose who we wish to be as adults. No longer do we feel trapped in endless cycles of painful acting out and acting in. We become more flexible, develop an ability to forgive ourselves, and release internalized shame about who we are. In short, we *heal* ourselves from the inside out by *reliving* feelings, *releasing* them and then *redeciding* how we *want* to relate to ourselves and others. We pump out the "bilge water" that has accumulated in the bottom of our psychological boat and are left with *space* to create and to discover the *power of being*.

A final note on feelings and the past versus the present. On our healing voyage we will be dealing both with old feelings and beliefs from the *past* and with new feelings and perspectives in the *present*. Much confusion can be avoided by understanding that the way to deal with the past and with the present needs to be different.

When confronted with feelings and beliefs stuck with from the past the goal is to relive, release and redecide. In the present, however, the goal is to live in such a manner that *prevents* negative feelings from accumulating within and/or to clearly express them. The former can be thought of as *uncovering* work while the latter as *artful living.* It is not denial or avoidance to discover a style of living in the present that eliminates hurtful conflicts and unhappy experiences.

The next chapter, the cornerstone of this book, discusses some of the specific internal perceptual and external behavioral changes that are likely to occur as a natural result of family origin work. We do not have to wait for all of the "bilge water" to be "pumped out" before adopting some of these new perceptions and behaviors.

CHAPTER SIX:
SETTING YOUR SAILS

FROM COMPULSIVE DOING TO HEALTHY BEING: SUGGESTIONS FOR THE JOURNEY

R eliving and releasing the buried feelings that fuel compulsive doing is an essential part of the process of recovering the power of being. In a sense, it allows us to re-write our history and detach from the messages we received that drive shoulds, perfectionism and obsessive-compulsive behavior. In essence, family of origin work allows us to heal compulsive doing from inside out.

Family of origin work involves and activates *feelings*. It is important to continually keep in mind that feelings are crucial in the healing process. Compulsive doers are often heavily invested in living the hero, caretaker, or people-pleaser roles. Heros tend not to show feelings. They hide their pain and needs away. The self-interventions suggested in this chapter all pale in comparison with the power of releasing our *feelings*. Breaking out of the hero role and letting go of the sense of inner shame that drives it can alter our whole manner of relating to ourself and others. When a leap of faith is taken to show ourself as a person with hurts and needs many of the changes suggested below just *naturally* begin to happen inside. As with any addictive, or compulsive behavior, it is the repression of feelings that drives compulsive doing.

Another path back to our power of being that can be employed, even while pursuing retrospective family of origin work, involves making direct choices to take care of ourselves in healthy ways during our daily life. Eventually as we come to understand and embrace what happened to us in our family of origin, we will naturally begin to take care of ourselves better in our current life. It isn't always necessary, however, to wait for this more long-term process of resolution to take place. Here and now we can begin to redesign our approach to daily living.

Employing the suggestions in this Chapter will have the effect of re-focusing on our own needs, feelings, choices, and awareness. This is crucial to regaining the power of being. *Compulsive doing*, as described from the outset of this book, arises from a tendency to focus on what we think we *should* be doing, saying, or accomplishing. *Healthy being* is a level of awareness, or a way of living life in which we listen to our spontaneous self and allow it to inform and guide us. Instead of controlling, caretaking, or projecting our needs and feelings outward on others and our environment, we re-focus inside to find our own disinhibited sense of *beingness*.

This journey, then, is very individual and unique. It is one that we must each embark on individually. Our journey is towards the recovery of that "spiritual and creative child" (Osbon, 1991) within us. No one can tell us how this journey is *supposed* to look for us. Only by listening to our inner voice that says, "This may not make any sense, but it is what I *feel* inside is right for me now" do we find our direction.

The reader is cautioned not to take the following suggestions too seriously. They only point the way and give permission to try out things you might not have thought of before. No one can tell you how your healing process *should* look. Letting go of that need to be told "how to do it" may be scary at times, but it is part of the essence of healing itself. Without the freedom to follow our inner light even the best of suggestions and techniques becomes another meaningless compulsive ritual!

In general we can begin this work through two avenues: Changing our *Internal* Lifestyle — or how we *view* or life; and Changing our *External* Lifestyle — or how we *live* our life.

First discussed will be changing internal perspectives, since external attempts at change (e.g., time management, reducing work hours, etc.) will be difficult to maintain without the healthy internal perspective (e.g., letting go of perfectionism, staying "centered," etc.) needed to support such outward alterations in lifestyle.

A word or two is in order regarding the suggestions presented below and how to use them. It's important to remember that when we make interventions such as these we are essentially re-parenting ourselves. We're recognizing unhealthy patterns, images, and behaviors that we have acquired during our development, or that are used to protect ourself from the pain we encountered as children. We are then changing those messages, replacing them with the affirming, healing messages that we needed to hear from our parents but didn't.

Again, remember that when we find ourselves acting out unhealthy patterns (such as compulsive doing) we can know that behind that behavior is a repressed *feeling* that needs to be honored, listened to, and expressed. If you are trying out some of the self-interventions suggested below and find they are not doing anything for you, you may need to go back and do more work with your feelings around that particular situation. Again, until we work through the *feelings* that *drive* our overworking, caretaking, contr ng, etc., we will tend to go back to them. why I have discussed family of origin work is book.)

o important to know that re-parenting kes lots and lots of practice. The road to ot one for the faint hearted! There are lots of reasons why it does not make *sense* to follow our inner voice.   We need to learn not to beat ourselves up about how much we beat ourselves up! We can be patient with ourselves. As we do so, the new messages and ways of being we are exploring gradually become part of us. Eventually, as when we learned to drive a car, the new ways of doing things become automatic. That may not happen for a while. It may not happen for a *long* time, but it will happen.

We need to be patient with ourselves — and keep practicing.   Try these suggestions out *at your own pace.* When you find something that works for you *stay with it!* Listen to that little voice inside of you that informs you and guides you. If you keep at it, little by little you will develop an internal lifestyle that arises out of your *beingness* and compulsive doing will seem less and less attractive. Decide which strategies work best for *you* and modify them to fit your personal needs. Then keep practicing.

CHANGING YOUR INTERNAL LIFESTYLE (PERSPECTIVES)

The following are some attitudes, perspectives, techniques, or ways of approaching life that seem to be helpful in recovering our individual *power of being.* Like everything new that we learn in life they require of us a willingness to practice and a certain degree of courage. Here we go.

Use Fear As A Compass

Like many of the concepts in this Chapter, this principle goes directly against the way that we usually do things in our society.

As you will recall from Chapter Three, fear is at the bottom of almost all human suffering. This is a sweeping statement, but very accurate when one begins to look at it closely. The problem is not the fear itself, but that we do not know how to *use* it in a healthy way for growth.

Fear can serve as a compass to *point the direction we need to go.* Although it may be our first impulse, the thing to do when afraid is not to run away from (or avoid) the circumstance, event, or person that we fear, but rather to move *into* that fear. This is different from controlling, changing, caretaking, or forcing. What we do is to embrace, accept, and view the fear as a teacher. We do not avoid it, nor surrender our identity to it, nor seek to control it. We *do* acknowledge it, embrace it, and stay on our course.

Back in early 1984 when first awakening to the issues of compulsive doing in my own life, I had been in the habit of going out to lunch to socialize with colleagues from work. As my life began to change, however, I found that I was drawn towards going to a certain park by myself to eat lunch on my car hood and just *be.* At the time many people told me this was an unhealthy sign and just one more indicator that I was "going off the deep end". My fear informed me that they were right and that I really *should* force myself to be socially outgoing and have lunch with my colleagues.

Fortunately, a good friend one day said simply, "If that is what your heart is telling you to do then you must do it in spite of your fears." I followed this advice and out of those long solitary lunches developed a sense of self-ownership and self-identity which then allowed me to be in relationships with people in a totally new and more centered way.

Life presents us with a continual parade of fears. The worst of these usually involve fears of rejection, or emotional/physical abandonment. If we use these fears as teachers and compasses to point the direction we need to go, we will grow proportionately stronger in our power of being. Look at your life right now. Where do you feel that there is a wall of fear in front of you preventing you from moving forward? *That* is the very direction your power of being lies in.

Do Nothing

If you are not able to feel good about yourself doing nothing, you are not ready to do something.

Compulsive doing is filled with paradoxes. And "doing nothing" is one of them. When we feel compulsive doing grabbing hold , when it seems that our strivings are getting out of control, the last thing it seems like we should do is nothing! Of course we want to do something, anything, to change or relieve the situation. If we can only figure out what we are doing "wrong" we can "fix" it — right?

Wrong! One of the most powerful interventions we can make with ourselves when our compulsive doing is flaring up is to actually, literally *do nothing*. Doing nothing in this sense means just that. How it works is to sit in your favorite spot (I find the hammock I installed on my front porch works well — at least during the summer.) Don't *do* anything. This means don't read. Don't do homework, Don't put the new band you bought on your watch. Don't talk on the phone. Don't watch television. *Do nothing!* Then just stay where you are even if you feel waves of anxiety, drivenness and tension crash over you. You may want to run away, but just stay with it and eventually those compulsive feelings will diminish enough for you to begin to *feel* again. Remind yourself that what you're doing is temporarily abstaining from your activity, doing, and shoulding. Admit that you *need* and deserve to stop hurting yourself by forcing yourself to do so much. Remind yourself that it's okay to do nothing sometimes and that other people do give themselves permission to do nothing sometimes. If it's okay for them, it's *certainly* okay for you.

Keep in mind that many people who are compulsive doers assume that more is better. We look for the "perfect" place, or circumstances to relax. We plod toward the weekend thinking that *then* we can finally relax. In reality, even *if* we finally get to that stopping spot we are so wound up it's all but impossible to let go and *be*.

When looking for the perfect situation to relax, we are setting out on an impossible quest. There *is* no "perfect" situation! We must learn to *be* right where we *are*. I personally cannot recall a time when I got everything "just right" and then was able to let go and feel serene. Instead I may end up with all the right "stuff" (sunny day, favorite book, soft sandy beach.) only to feel frustrated and uptight. Some of the best non-compulsive-doing times, on the other hand, often happen at the most unlikely moments — in parking lots, driving between appointments, painting the house. Compulsive doing is an "addiction" to *external* circumstances which we try to control or caretake. More of the same focusing on externals just gets us more stuck.

When we "do nothing" we are actually doing something very important. We are shifting from doing to being. This eventually brings us back to ourselves, which is what we've been missing all along. We usually try to solve compulsive doing with more work. We attend seminars on stress management, we read more and more books, we plan vacations and we shift our schedules around for the thirteenth, or the thirtieth time. All of this activity drives us deeper into our addiction and gives us more tasks we "should" do.

Stay with the "do nothing" exercise for as much time as necessary. It sometimes takes a few hours, or we find we need to keep doing the exercise repeatedly over days or weeks. Be honest. Listen to yourself. There will be signs when you are beginning to feel connected with yourself and "back in your body" again. It will be apparent when you have finally shifted gears from a human doing to a human being again. Then, gradually, slowly, and without losing touch with your inner pacing, begin to resume your activities for the day.

It may also be helpful *after* practicing this exercise to write notes about what you experienced. (For example, feelings you may have been pushing down through compulsive doing may surface.) Doing nothing can teach us much about ourselves — if we're willing to listen.

This quote from Franz Kafka (John-Roger, 1991) may be helpful while you practice "doing nothing": "You do not need to leave your room. Remain sitting at your table and listen. Do not even listen, simply wait. Do not even wait, be quite still and solitary. The world will freely offer itself to you to be unmasked, it has no choice, it will roll in ecstasy at your feet!"

A Silent Day

Similar to the *Do Nothing* exercise is the *Silent Day*. This is an extremely powerful method to release unhealthy control of and attachment to surroundings and other people. One of the primary ways in which humans tend to seek control over surroundings is through language. We dictate, whine, obsess, ruminate, worry fret, rage, argue, and otherwise convince ourselves that we need to change what is around us in order to be happy. Being silent for a time is an abrupt and powerful reminder that we have the power to let go, lighten up, release, and disinhibit from compulsive doing and shoulding *without* anyone, or anything around us giving us permission to change, or changing with or for us.

In our society being silent for a whole day often presents difficulties, but not ones which cannot be surmounted. I recommend that you type a business-size card which says, "Greetings. I am choosing not to talk today as a form of personal growth. While I cannot talk to you I would be happy to interact with you in other ways and you are welcome to talk to me. Thank you for your understanding." This can help to smooth the passage through the day.

It is helpful to enlist the aid of family and friends. Let them know what you are going to be doing. Tell them that occasional note writing is allowed, but tends to take away from the value of the exercise. Ask them to run interference if any sales people come to the door, or the phone rings. Invite them to *participate* with you and not to avoid you just because you are not talking.

It can be fun to do a silent day *with* other people. You will be likely to notice your relationships actually *deepening* in your silence. Perceptions and feelings toward others and our relationships to them are largely based on what goes on *inside of us*. When we love ourselves we begin to feel lovingly towards others. When we accept ourselves we are free to accept others. A day of silence brings us alive to our natural inside self and helps to disconnect from the illusion that it is what and who is outside of us that "makes" us feel the way we do.

Facing It Down

Compulsive doing can be like a wild tiger! Sometimes the best thing to do is simply to "face it down." We remind ourself that where we are and what we are doing is *okay*, that we are *okay*, and that our surroundings do not control us. In short — we turn and face ourselves, and say "This is where my compulsive doing is going to stop.".

It is important to understand what is meant by this, since it *is* different from "Do Nothing" and other techniques presented here. Compulsive doers are deeply enmeshed with the environment. The problem is an overdeveloped desire to control. We have learned to control our surroundings, or at least to feel like we are. Ironically, of course, we begin to eventually feel that it controls us.

We may, for example, be at a restaurant and feel we don't have a right to exist, as if the surroundings have some power over us. We somehow feel we must stay active and "in control" or we are not okay.

Facing down is *giving ourselves the right to be where we are* (eg. eating in a restaurant) and telling ourself that over and over, and letting it sink in. Slowly, we begin to feel less controlled by compulsive behavior and surroundings, and feel more self-possessed and spontaneous. A helpful "facing down" self-statement can be, "This is just me here. It does

not matter where I am. I carry me with me. I have
the power to be myself right now and the right to
exist in this time and place. I can stop doing and just
be. I am okay."

Surrender

It is no accident that the first step in the
Alcoholics Anonymous program is *admitting* that one
is addicted and that life has become "unmanageable".
Often compulsive doers need to do this also. We need
to surrender to the reality of our compulsiveness.

Compulsive doers are often in the "hero" role and
heroes carry a great deal of shame, which makes it
hard to admit to anything less than perfection. We
do, however, need to admit our powerlessness. We
sometimes need to say to ourselves (and often to
someone else as well) that things are out of control —
that our compulsive lifestyle has become
unmanageable. That process of admitting to our
compulsive doing helps us to detach from it; to begin
to see that we are *not* our compulsion to doing —
that we are *not* what we do. It allows us to begin to
be again.

The concept of surrender also extends to not
forcing ourselves. Forcing our way through life is
second nature for many compulsive doers. We have
an amazing ability to push ourselves to do more and
be more than is healthy. We even may attempt to
extend this philosophy of "more is better" to our
healing process.

Healing from compulsive doing, however, comes not through forcing, but through acceptance, slowing down, and relaxing. Less IS more, particularly in our journey back to healthy being. Often the best thing we can do for ourselves is to let go and let life sneak up on us. The idea is to keep saying "I'm just going to let this moment happen to me right now." When we do that we tend to be drawn into the spontaneity of what is going on around us, which as compulsive doers is where we want to be. Life flows freely when we do not control it so much. In this sense, less is more fun.

Surrendering and not forcing things can be a little unsettling at first. One "advantage" to compulsive doing is that things become predictable and routine. When we are approaching life compulsively there is little opportunity for unexpected events, feelings, or awarenesses to occur. We need to be prepared for this to change when we lighten up and let in the present moment. We will find that there is a whole stream of life going on that we do not usually experience — but is nonetheless going on all around us. When we stop forcing, we open up to the *experience* of the moment which can be both wonderful and unsettling.

Say "NO" to Shoulds

Shoulds are the arch enemy of the compulsive doer. Shoulds separate us from ourselves and drive us to sell out in relationships, activities, and spiritual growth. I have never had a situation in adult life where shoulds helped me out. Even when the shoulds are helping to accomplish some glorious task, in the end there is emptiness, confusion, and an inner loss rendering any accomplishment unsatisfying.

Saying "no" to shoulds can be very simple, but we often make it complicated. We need to *stop* what we are doing and ask, "Is this what I want to be doing right now? Does this feel connected to my inner pacing/flow? Is it coming from inside of me, or from an externally imposed sense of obligation or duty?" If the answer is "yes" then keep up the good work. If the answer is "no" then it's time to let go of shoulds. Shoulding on ourselves automatically gets us lost. Letting go of shoulds helps us center on who we are.

Forgive Yourself

As discussed in the section on family of origin work, one of the powerful messages compulsive doers received as children was that there is "no forgiveness". We may have internalized this message as we were wondering why our father didn't seem to want to be around us. We may have internalized this message when we were listening to our parents arguing and it seemed they had little empathy for one another. We may have internalized this message from teachers who may have praised us for successes but failed to praise us for just being *who* we were. As adults we tend to use all of these messages on ourselves just as we were shown how to as children.

Forgiving ourselves as compulsive doers means letting go of internalized shame about messages like those above. It also means letting go of our tendency

to judge ourselves harshly for the things we have
done. It also means forgiving ourselves for what we
have *not* done. As compulsive doers we often feel
that we should do everything and that we should do
it *now*! We decided that the way to avoid getting
abandoned was to work hard and achieve to prove
ourselves. When we are not achieving we often feel
worthless and non-existent.   Forgiveness for
compulsive doers is saying "It's okay for me to just be
alive today, right now! It's okay for me to live, to
feel, to be, to *exist*!" Forgive yourself now — you are
worth it!

Affirm Yourself

There are a tremendous number of books of
affirmations on the market right now. There is a
good reason for this. Affirmations are a form of
parenting that we can do for ourselves as adults.
Affirmations are one way we can learn to care for
ourselves, develop healthy perspectives, and shift our
focus to a more healing outlook. Affirmations are a
medium through which we can hear and internalize
the messages that we needed to hear as children, but
didn't.

Read through some of the affirmation books
available. There are even a few available now in the
area of compulsive doing. Choose one that feels like
a good fit and then use it. It is helpful to read an
affirmation each day and then dive into several that
really hit home at times when you are struggling with
your compulsive doing the most.

It is also very powerful to write your own affirmations. A number of years ago when I was struggling with giving myself permission to separate from (and eventually leave) my job, I had an affirmation on my office bulletin board that said "You own you". This simple statement, repeated over and over, eventually helped me to develop the strength needed to make a powerful shift in the direction of my life. Design your own affirmations to address the negative messages you have internalized (as you become aware of them in your family of origin work). Post them where they will work best for you. When you see them breathe deeply, relax, and let the words sink into your being.

Let Go of Guilt

Guilt can serve a healthy function in its place. It keeps us from getting into trouble and hurting others. Unfortunately it also drives much of our obsessive-compulsive behavior. It is essential that we begin to discriminate between real guilt and false guilt. When we find ourselves feeling guilty and wanting to soothe that guilt, what we need to do is not work harder and harder, but let go of the guilt that's driving us. When we see how destructive guilt has been in our lives and how much it can and has damaged our relationships, letting it go becomes the only sensible thing to do.

Avoid "Staring" at Yourself

As compulsive doers we have a peculiar tendency to focus obsessively on ourselves. Not that we are being selfish. Far from it! What we are actually doing is picking ourselves apart for any flaws, or chinks in the armor. We can even develop a nasty tendency to hyper-evaluate ourself regarding our compulsive doing. "Oh no, there I go again shoulding on myself" we say and then begin to mercilessly analyze our behavior, getting more and more externalized all the time as we do so.

Staring at ourselves makes it difficult to be spontaneous and alive. We feel like a bug under a microscope and become more and more constricted and uptight. When we catch ourselves "staring," we can shift our focus to giving ourselves *permission* to let go again. It helps to remember that we need to focus on what we want to be *right* in life — not what is *wrong*. Focusing on what's "wrong" just seems to bring more of the same. Usually what we need is not to "figure it out", but to disinhibit ourselves and let go. That allows our energy to flow more freely while we let God (or our higher power) handle the figuring out for us.

Disinhibit Yourself

Spontaneity is one of the main outcomes of the healing process from compulsive doing. As repeatedly mentioned, compulsive doing is a process of externalizing our focus to the point where we end up living for goals and expectations that are outside of us. Disinhibiting means letting our energy flow again. Disinhibiting is an emotional *and* physical experience in which we release the rigid control that we impose on ourselves. Disinhibiting invariably brings greater access to our spirituality.

Describing the process of disinhibiting in words is very difficult since it is a psychophysical, or mind and body, experience. The easiest way to access the quality of disinhibition is to physically let go and release our bodies to move as they want. This sends a powerful message to the rest of our emotional and mental being. Moving to music, dancing, tapping, gesturing freely, making love, or just accepting our bodies and the feedback it gives us awakens our disinhibition process. It is that quality of self-acceptance we are looking for when we disinhibit.

The place to start practicing disinhibition is right here in the now. There is an aliveness waiting to spring up from inside. Our job is to coax it out by being willing to let go of our excessive need to be in control. Often our disinhibition comes out when we are simply not doing much. Inhibition on the other hand thrives on complexity, forcing, and compulsiveness. Disinhibition comes naturally to fill the space created in your life when you let go of such negative behaviors. Disinhibition is the reward for facing down the fear we have of not being acceptable to ourself or others when we don't give in to shoulds.

When you have experienced disinhibition (and most of us have at one time or another) a life of shoulds pales by comparison! The actual *experience* of letting ourselves not be "perfect" and risking letting go of our cautions and conservative ideas of what others think and expect of us is incredibly powerful. It leads to a wild and natural grace in living in which our sleep becomes sweet. Our laugh becomes easy and flowing. Our anger evaporates. Play becomes more attractive than work. Our bodies relax and release. We are more expressive with our physicality (including sexually). We become open to emotional risk. Our face brightens. Life takes on a sensual quality.

Focus Forward

Healing from compulsive doing can be a difficult task at times. It is easy to get caught up in focusing on what we do not want (the problems) rather than what we do want (the solutions). This is especially true since our fear makes us think that it is safer to sit back and complain about what *is* rather than take the difficult risks to *change* things. Especially for compulsive doers the lure of the negative is very strong.

While not ignoring the fact that there may indeed be a great deal of pain and struggle in our lives, *it is always best to focus towards what we want and not on what we do not want.* This approach of "thinking forward" leads towards the solutions we need to actually move forward.

Remember The Power of Choice

One thing that can be very powerful in recovering our power of being is to acknowledge the reality that we are constantly "at choice" in life. Life is, at it's essence, entirely optional. Ultimately, if you think about it, we don't even have to stay alive if we don't want. Yet so many of us live as if everything we get into is a should and a must.

The point of this is not to make ourselves into suicidal kamikazes, but rather to bring home the truth that we are *choosing* what we do in life. That realization puts us back into the driver's seat so we can experience self-ownership again. Life works best when we know who's in charge. When we give our power away to other people and circumstances, we experience ourselves as helpless and at the effect of our surroundings. When we realize that everything we do is a choice (even when it is between two not so positive options) we regain our power to be.

Feel Your Voice

This is another one of those strange-sounding strategies, but one that really works. You may have already noticed that when you are in touch with your spontaneous power of being side, you are able to smile, laugh, and express yourself more freely and naturally. We can also use this awareness in the reverse to remind us when we are getting off the being track and moving too deeply into our compulsive doing mode.

One of the first things we may notice when we are forcing, shoulding, and being compulsive is that our voice takes on a quality of deadness. Also, our laughter may become forced, or disappear altogether. By listening to our voice and becoming aware that this is happening we can take time out, slow down and start asking helpful questions: "What do I need right now?"; "How am I feeling *really?*"; "What can I do to re-connect with myself?"

Often when we stop ourselves like this we find there is a degree of anger in the background. This is a natural result of having pushed ourselves too far and done too much. Anger can be used in a helpful way as a warning signal that we are getting too far into shoulds and losing touch with our spontaneity.

Be Willing To Change

It is surprising how strongly we cling to routine and repetition. Part of our basic wiring seems to be a desire to have things remain as constant as possible. We resist change, even when it is for the better. When we are on a positive growth path, however, we need to be willing to have things change to some degree, or they won't.

On a day-to-day basis, we can benefit by being willing to allow for flexibility in our schedule. We do well to strive to stay continually in touch with what we want to do and not what we think we should do. We may have decided the night before what our next day was going to look like. Many of us then proceed to carry through with the scheduled activities even if we don't feel like it. That is a mistake and takes us away from our power of being. To whatever extent it is possible in our personal circumstances it is important to listen to our feelings and make alterations in our plans in accord with the feedback we are getting from inside.

This principle holds true even in relaxation activities. Thus, I may have planned to go for a bike ride with my spouse or friend on my day off and, when the time arrives, instead sit on my porch and rest. When we are being responsive to our inner rhythms, changes in plans will become natural and frequent occurrences. It's okay to be flexible and let go into what feels right now.

Beware of Making Sense

One way of approaching life that tends to decrease our flexibility is always doing what it "makes sense" to do. For example, we may decide we would like to run a particular errand which fits with our current needs and energy level. Just before we leave the house we are reminded that "as long as we are going that way" there are two or three other errands that "need" to be done. In accepting the additional tasks, we run out of time and end up rushing to get everything done. Our initial errand then also becomes a should and we return home without having enjoyed any part of the trip — but we did "accomplish" three times what we had planned! Or did we?

If we continue to live our lives out of this "sensible" approach can you see what will happen? Eventually we will arrive at the end of our time on this planet and they will write on our tombstone, "She got a great many things accomplished - too bad none of it was any fun!" Even though we may have to do battle with our feeling of guilt and fears of rejection it is crucial to learn that not everything has to make sense. In fact, if we are doing what it "makes sense" to do it is usually a tip-off that our power of being lies elsewhere.

Lighten Up!

Along with disinhibition comes a feeling of "lightening up". Compulsive doers are some of the most serious people around. Our abandonment and rejection fears drive us to an intensity few people can match. When we are able to take a "bigger view", to adopt a healthier perspective on our lives (e.g., "Will what I am doing now really *matter* in the long run? Is it important enough to be printed on my tombstone?") we begin to see the humor. We can even begin to find humor in our own compulsive doing. As we lighten up we also detach, letting go of the feeling that everything we do is so very important.

It is less helpful to *try* to *do* something funny than it is to *be* funny. It seems to be a process of letting go, right now in this moment, and letting our natural humor rise to the surface. It is more a process of *not suppressing* our humor than of pretending to be funny. Life itself is funny when we get out of its way.

Lightening up also means something even more spiritual. When we let go of the idea that everything we do *matters*, life paradoxically becomes richer and fuller. We learn that life is a process that requires a light touch to be lived well. For example, have you ever noticed that the more you try to control your spouse, significant other, or children, the more they tend to rebel and oppose you? When we simply take a humorous and light hearted approach, people tend to have less difficulty working along side us cooperatively. As we loosen our strangle-hold on life, the energy around and within begins to flow more freely. Things develop with less effort and become more playful.

Feeling the Feelings

When we're feeling our feelings we're not acting out compulsive doing. We may wish we were since feelings are not always pleasant (especially the "big three" — fear, anger, and hurt). In the long run, however, we are better off when we let the feelings come up, acknowledge them, and express them openly. Compulsive doers grow up with messages about being strong and heroic and not being "selfish". Acknowledging our feelings can be viewed as a weakness, or self-indulgence — something we do not like to entertain.

The moment we begin acting out our compulsive doing is the very time we most need to stop what we're doing and listen to ourselves. What is my body telling me? Are my muscles tight with fear and anxiety? Does my jaw ache with anger? Is this ache in my upper chest sadness that I am not wanting to feel? Stopping obsessive-compulsive behavior and listening is in itself a strong statement of our willingness to embrace who we are and to begin to love ourselves. When feeling stuck and off track, always look at what you are *feeling*. It may take a while to identify, but it's worth the effort.

Sharing feelings is absolutely crucial to the healing process. To do so often requires a leap of faith. We fear that we will lose our self-esteem and the respect of others if we show pain, need, hurt, or responsible anger. Actually quite the opposite is true. *In one moment we can change our whole perspective on life if we trust ourself enough to release our feelings.* When we do we are making the statement that we are not the perfect heroes who can get it all done and force our way through any situation. To let others see chinks in our emotional armor is to break the cycle of compulsivily proving we can do it all, all of the time.

Let Go of Perfection

Another favorite pastime of compulsive doers is tormenting ourselves with trying to be "perfect". Somewhere along the line, we've internalized an image of flawlessness that can make it all but impossible to even exist. Perfection is a kind of living purgatory that we put ourselves in — and can get ourselves out of too.

One way of getting out of the perfection trap is to try not to succeed. Even just saying "I don't know" can be liberating for the obsessive-compulsive perfectionist. We may also be surprised at other people's reactions. Instead of being rejected and abandoned as we had feared, others may begin to treat us like humans! They may experience a sense of relief that they can "let their hair down" and not push themselves so hard to keep up with us. Then *we* can enjoy playing together and just being normal folks.

Stop Beating Yourself Up About Beating Yourself Up!

Oh, boy! This is a twisted idea! How many times a day do we find ourselves saying not-so-nice things about how we have handled our time and energies? This is especially true when we first begin to become aware of our compulsive doing and start recovering. During these initial weeks and months we often will "catch" ourselves acting out compulsive doing. Even when we have the best intentions to "take some time for myself", or to "just relax and take things easy" we will still frequently find ourselves doing, shoulding, and accomplishing.

When this happens it is important not to make things worse by beating ourselves over the head about it. For example, I have frequently taken a day off for myself and found that, no matter how hard I worked at it, I ended up over-scheduling, driving myself to accomplish more than my inner sensibilities told me was good for me, and basically ended up miserable and tired. This is not unusual for obsessive-compulsive people. Sometimes we console ourselves by saying, "At least we got some things done" but inside we feel disappointed in ourselves and our tendency to relapse.

We can learn to stop wherever we are in the relapse process, to pat ourself on the back for "at least catching it" before we got too crazed, and then slowly get in touch again with our inner rhythm and needs. This approach is better than getting more tense and upset with ourselves.

Ask Your Higher Power

As compulsive doers we need to be able to admit when things become unmanageable. We need to be able to ask God, or our "higher power", such as we perceive him, her, or it, for help. Like all addictions, compulsive doing involves an unhealthy amount of denial and pride. We feel that *we* are in control and that all we need is just a little more accomplished before we can rest. Hopefully, before our bodies and relationships collapse, we come to a place where we are exhausted and hurting enough that we can reach out for help.

One helpful way to admit we can't do it alone is through use of "The Lifestyle Monitor" presented in Chapter Four. The "Lifestyle Monitor" can help show which areas are out of balance and to what extent. It provides a wonderful tool for assessing our needs. We can then share these needs with God and let God have a chance to work in our life.

Listen to Your Destiny

This may sound like something Yoda would say to Luke Skywalker in the movie "Star Wars", but it actually has a great deal of down-to-earth application. Each of us has a destiny and direction we are traveling in life. The people we meet, the careers we choose, everything in life seems to be part of a larger plan of which we have no knowledge.

If we approach life in this way, we will be less likely to want to control since we realize our destiny ultimately *cannot* be controlled. We will also be less judgemental and serious about our so-called "mistakes" since we know they are all part of the plan which is out of our hands anyway.

Living out a sense of destiny can be a huge relief for a perfectionistic compulsive doer who feels that every choice has to be the right one. It can be relaxing to let go and trust that things are turning out the way that they were meant to in life — even when we do not understand why.

Beware of Turning Being into Doing

Compulsive doers are very good at being active and taking action. We like to make things happen in the world. We express ourselves by creating, constructing, and achieving goals. That can be a wonderful asset or a terrible liability depending on how much balance we have between doing and being.

As we start our journey toward finding our power of being, many of us are tempted to institutionalize what we have learned. We want to take action on our discoveries. We want everyone to join us in a silent day. We decide to work more time to fit "do nothing" into our schedule.

What can happen, however, is that we lose touch with that all-important quality of spontaneous *being* that we were seeking. The power that comes from being cannot be forced, directed, limited, or structured. We may wake up on our scheduled silent day and find that every instinct within us says this is not the right day to spend in silence. We must be willing to listen to that inner guidance system. If we do not, we can spend years doing all the "right" things and never get closer to the sense of beingness. As is the case in developing our sense of "destiny", we find our awareness of being through *listening* not in legislating or forcing.

Let Go of the Future

This idea has been mentioned briefly, but it really deserves its own category. Compulsive doers are continually striving and moving *toward* something, even if it doesn't make sense and even if all resources are already exhausted. Recovery requires us to start focusing on the here and now. After all, the future may never get here! In this physical world we have no assurances of continued survival beyond right now. It only makes sense to live in this moment and in this moment alone.

Neil Diamond has a wonderful song called "Done Too Soon" in which he notes that all of us have one thing in common and that is the quality of our human experience. To "sweat beneath the same sun" and "look up in wonder at the same moon" is the essence of life — not all our grandiose abstract projects and plans! The real meat of life is here and now. It is feelings, sensations and the ability to experience the environment.

An interesting story came to me through an old friend, George Lewis, which illustrates this point. A Zen master was on his deathbed. His students rallied about him wanting to know the meaning of life before he passed on to the next one. Surely if anyone knew, this venerable old master did! Overcome by their pleas, the Zen master agreed to share with them the secret of the meaning of life, but *only* after they had brought him his last request, a piece of chocolate cake. The students rushed out and brought him back a huge piece of chocolate cake which he proceeded to gobble down with much fervor. When he was finished his students again asked him to tell them the meaning of life. The old master set his cake plate aside, looked at his assembled disciples and said "That was great cake!" Those were his final words.

Accept Everything

One of the great laws of the universe is that we acquire *more* of whatever we resist. When we argue with our spouse or lover that he/she doesn't "care" about us enough and should be "closer", they instead will withdraw, defend themselves, and argue. *What we resist invariably grows stronger and achieves more power over us.*

To demonstrate this principle, have a partner stand and push against your outstretched hands. The harder you push, the harder they push back, and so you in turn push harder. The eventual result is a collapse or breakdown of one of the parties.

In compulsive doing we are in a very real way resisting *life*. Instead of letting ourselves go with the flow, we are intent upon having it our way. This leads to resisting the way things actually are. We get more and more drained of our power in an effort to control.

Instead of resisting "accept everything". (This has become one of my personal favorite sayings!) Although, on the face of it, life often seems unacceptable, embracing what is around us gives greater power rather than less. It takes practice, but we *can* maintain boundaries, state needs and rights clearly, and *not* relinquish our sense of acceptance and "going with the flow".

Thomas Crum, author of *The Magic of Conflict* (1987) describes this process. Crum suggests that even when life is difficult and traumatic we can still maintain the open and receptive perspective of the learner. When accepting everything, we are not necessarily giving negative things our "approval", but we are willing to stop controlling, changing, and manipulating and to embrace things *as they are*. When in doubt, try a little acceptance!

Finding Your River

Acceptance (and many of the other suggestions presented here) can give a clearer sense of ourselves. One way to conceptualize this is "finding your own river".

Obsessive-compulsive behavior leads to feeling that things are forced, are requiring more energy than needed, and feeling cheated out of something. What you are being cheated out of is yourself, or what might be called your "river" of life. Picture standing and looking at two rivers flowing away into the distance. On the right is the river that you are *meant* to be in naturally and instinctively. This is the river of your life, your feelings, your needs. The name of this river is "Want To". The river on the left is the river you are *not* meant to be in. This river is one where you have to force yourself along. You have to struggle to keep up with the current. You do not feel welcome, but there is a sense of drivenness to "get somewhere". This is the river named "Should".

When we are operating out of compulsive doing we are in the river "Should". We are forcing ourselves. When we begin to *accept* ourselves, others, and situations, we make what is often a dramatic shift over into the river "Want To". We feel alive again, and in tune with life. It feels great! Then we run up against a rock! Encountering a rock is bad enough, but the real problem is that, instead of acknowledging that an obstacle was hit and moving on around it, we *resist* it. We find ourselves heading back into the river "Should" again.

As a compulsive doer it is very easy to find the way back to the river "Should". In moving towards *being*, however, we sense our own natural river "Want To". We develop an instinct for a more natural way of being. Eventually we are able to seek out and remain in our own river with greater and greater ease.

The Thinking Trap

Thought stoppage is a technique utilized by counselors working in the area of stress management (Davis, et al, 1982). When practicing thought stoppage, we are literally doing just that — stopping thoughts. In compulsive doing this can be very helpful. For example: we notice that there are some papers on our desk relating to things that need to be accomplished. Then we begin thinking about several of the projects that these papers will lead into. Next we start worrying about how to re-shuffle our schedule so there is time to do those projects. Eventually we begin to feel overwhelmed and anxious.

In thought stoppage, as soon as there is awareness of an obsessive-compulsive train of thought, begin to gently work our way backward. Starting with the current thoughts about schedule re-shuffling, trace your thoughts back to where they initially started, in this case the papers on the desk. Then allow yourself to become aware of something on the desk that would be more relaxing and nurturing to focus on. Instead focus on the picture of your spouse and loving family that was taken on vacation. Then begin to recall a pleasant event from that trip, and so on.

By utilizing thought stoppage mental activity can be re-trained. Gradually more and more time is spent thinking about healthy, relaxing and permission-giving things. As more time is spent thinking these thoughts, we will begin to *act* on more of them since there are more of them. The end result of thought stoppage can be an increase in self-care behaviors.

Be Willing to Change

Compulsive doers are nothing if not dedicated and dogged about life. We will continue to pursue a goal or activity even after others have long ago become exhausted and dropped unconscious! In making plans (even relaxation/recreation plans) we stick to our schedule because that's what we "should" do.

There are times when dogged determination can be a big help. Sometimes it takes dogged determination to get through that last exam, or mail the taxes on time. But living like a dog is for the birds! What we want is a little bit of pleasure and fun. It's hard to be or have fun when we are unable to be spontaneous and take what life offers *as it comes to us*. In order to do that we need to be willing to change. When a plan is made with a friend to go to dinner and a movie and things are running late due to an unscheduled appointment, be willing to shift gears. Call the friend and suggest meeting at Burger Knave instead of the Ritz so that there is time to eat and get to the movie without rushing.

How simple to say, but how difficult to allow ourselves to be flexible. How often we find ourselves scurrying around to fit everything in or get everything done. We end up frazzled, late, and with everyone angry. If we look at our life and find this to be the case more often than not, it's time to change our attitude toward change.

Say "So What"

Saying "So what" allows us to detach from our overly serious nature and realize the cosmic insignificance of most of our efforts. It brings to mind the saying "Don't sweat the small stuff...and it's all small stuff!" This is especially helpful when thinking that everything that we are doing is of GREAT importance.

It may be useful is to say the phrase "So what" after every "important" event or interaction. After we get the hang of it the voice inside begins to sound like, "Well, I just got stuck in traffic and am going to be late for that meeting and *so what*." That "so what" is a reminder that in the larger scheme of things this particular meeting and the five minutes missed is not going to change the fate of the Western world.

Compulsive doers may be saying, "But...if we *all* took such a cavalier attitude toward life there would be no one to be *responsible*!" It is important to understand that this suggestion is not being directed to a group of procrastinators, or a gang of antisocial psychopaths! Compulsive doers as a group tend to be *overly* responsible. When a work-aholic practices saying "so what" the net effect is simply to tone down an over-developed sense of responsibility. Strive to reach a level of responsibility that is healthy and more normal.

Lower Your Expectations

Perhaps this should be called having realistic expectations. Obsessive-compulsive folks tend to demand so much of themselves that others can only sit in awe (or shock!) In the process of recovery we begin to see that it just isn't realistic to expect ourselves to do as much as we've been doing. After all, what we are after is more time to *be* our spontaneous self. To do that we need to have less time and energy wrapped up in *doing*.

In the early stages of compulsive doing recovery, it is recommended to decrease the amount done each day by twenty percent. It is a continual process of re-deciding priorities during the day. For example, while driving to work decide not to pick up the dry cleaning since it can be done on the weekend. Once at the office, decide not to write the memo to the personnel office since it isn't due until next Wednesday. Then there is a few minutes extra to drive at a more leisurely pace and to even have a quick chat with a friend before the first meeting of the day.

People report that doing less actually seems like more in the long run. When we are not *forcing* ourselves so much to "get it all done", our lives seem more fulfilling and on-balance. Also, we will not be so continually fatigued that things are forgotten and need to be done over.

Stay "Centered"

"Centering" is a psychophysiological technique which has been developed through the disciplines of yoga and the martial arts (Tohei, 1980; Crum, 1987). It is wonderfully helpful when attempting to re-focus internally rather than being caught up in, or reactive to, outside influences. For compulsive doers this technique is an easy-to-use tool for de-escalating an obsessive-compulsive crisis and bringing back a sense of inner needs and rhythms.

In order to "center" focus attention on the exact geographic middle of your physical body. That is a point an inch or two below the navel and in the center of the abdomen. Just as you can hold out your hand in front of you and feel the sensation of opening and closing our fingers (try it) you can "feel" this center point in your body.

Once a sense of this center point of physical anatomy is developed, it can be used as an intervention in times of stress, crisis, and when we are wrapped up in compulsive doing. By focusing on this center point, attention shifts inward and internal balance gets reestablished.

In order to "test" your centered state, ask someone to give you a gentle push on the shoulder while standing side by side with you. If your body wobbles you are not centered. If you feel a sense of solidness and stability you have mastered the centered state. As with all healthy behaviors, we need to keep practicing.

As we focus on this center point something very interesting happens. We being to sense our energies returning to where they naturally should be within us. We begin to think about how to take care of ourself rather than doing and shoulding. We make "I" statements (see page 135) and focus on our own needs rather than blaming and projecting onto others. We find a balanced wholeness instead of reacting to the "fight/flight" instinct. Centering provides a *physical metaphor for self-ownership and the experience of being.*

The Power of Relaxation

Our culture gives the less-than-helpful message that we need to become *tense* in a crisis. No matter if that "crisis" is only a service station attendant forgetting to return a credit card, or a favorite television show being pre-empted by a big-time wrestling special. In our culture, tension, at some level or another, is often the state in which many exist from morning to night. Unfortunately, tension *never* really helps. In fact, we are more "prepared" to handle both short- and long-term crises and stresses when feeling relaxed and at peace.

Many compulsive doers have, in their childhood backgrounds, histories of abuse or neglect. We deal with abuse and neglect by *contracting* away from the pain. The pattern of contraction leads away from ourselves and teaches us to shut down, close up, and deny our feelings. Relaxation does the opposite. It leads to showing others our feelings (especially pain) and to embrace life as it is rather than controlling or caretaking it.

It is important for compulsive doers to *carry with them a belief in the power of relaxation*. When truly believing that relaxation is the best choice, we are healthier, happier, and more able as people. At the same time, we're more likely to opt for relaxation even in times of true crisis and stress. The next time you become tense, listen to the voice of relaxation inside and then let go!

Be Willing To Be Vulnerable

Vulnerability is actually strength in disguise. This is a major paradox in life for compulsive doers. Acting out compulsive doing demonstrats our invulnerability through our control. When being vulnerable, we "admit" that we're not perfect (and that only God can control everything).

Being vulnerable means opening up. It means telling those *little truths* that happen each moment of the day. It means letting people *see* what is going on inside and not rigidly adhering to a false image of strength. It means letting go and letting the real self out. Being vulnerable is risky and brave and one of the most difficult things done as humans. It is also one of the most life-giving and is a powerful antidote for compulsive doing.

"*Embrace The Tiger*"

This wonderful phrase embodies the concept of embracing conflict as opportunity for growth, healing and change (Crum, 1987). It also makes good practical survival sense. When approached by a tiger (stress) in life, we can choose to turn and run, in which case the tiger is very likely to bite us on the butt. We can charge screaming at the tiger and get our head chewed off or, we can remain calm and centered and give the tiger a hug! (Tigers need affection too, you know.) When we embrace the tiger we may find that he (stress) is a powerful friend and ally!

When confronted by a situation at work or at home which you would normally "attack" into or "run away" from (getting compulsive doing activated in the process), try "embracing" it. Slow down, take your time, discover what the situation has to teach you. Do some observing. Write out your thoughts. Look at how you can move *into* the crisis, getting close enough to use the energy it brings with it for growth and healing. There is almost always a way to do that if we look close enough.

Let Go of Caretaking and Controlling

It is fitting to end this section where compulsive doing begins. Compulsive doing, as I have pointed out earlier, is largely about caretaking others and controlling the environment. When engaging in these behaviors, however, we lose more and more self-ownership and identity.

What we need to do instead is let ourselves off the hook. We need to be willing to see that caretaking and controlling are not helpful to others or ourselves. We need to be willing to stop what we're doing and remind ourselves to "let go and let God" instead of playing at being God. We need to remind ourselves that we don't need to fix others, that we are not responsible for them. We don't need to get everything accomplished and in perfect order.

When we do this our natural self comes out again and sponaneity returns. Then, and only then, do we truly have something to give to others and to the world.

The following is a list of 15 common statement that compulsive doers often seem to have internalized from their family of origin. You may recognize some of these messages and can probably think of many more. After each of the messages are one or two of the areas outlined in this section as an antidote to the negative message.

1. "I must always be perfect in order to be okay. I am not valuable the way I naturally am."
   RX: Accept Everything

2. "Being prepared or tense helps to make things work out. If I'm tense I'll be more ready to handle things."
   RX: Disinhibit Yourself; The Power of Relaxation

3. "I need to be stressed in order to show I care."

RX: Lighten Up; Say No to Shoulds; Do Nothing

4. "I am responsible for other people and things."
   RX: Let   Go   of   Guilt;   Let   Go   of
   Caretaking/Controlling

5. "External things/people determine who I am.
Things outside of me will make me happy and
satisfied.
   RX: Center; Affirm Yourself; Silent Day

6. "Others' opinions of me determine me."
   RX: Find Your River; Affirm Yourself

7. "Life is about achievement. I must live for the
future and achieve as much as possibe."
   RX: Let   Go   of   Perfection;   Lower   Your
   Expectations.

8. "Avoiding feelings will make them go away."
   RX: Feel Your Feelings; Find Your River

9. "The mind and the body are separate. It doesn't
really matter what I feel, just so I get things done."
   RX: Lighten Up; Disinhibit Yourself

10.   "I must understand and control my life to
find happiness."
   RX: Ask Your Higher Power; Accept Everything

11.   "Being vulnerable is dangerous. Others do
not want to see what I am feeling. I have no right to
burden them."

RX: Let Go of Caretaking/Controlling; Be Vulnerable

12.   "Relationships are a matter of compromise."
RX: Silent Day; Center; Embrace the Tiger

13.   "Conflict is bad and should be avoided whenever possible."
RX: Embrace the Tiger; Accept Everything

14.   "I can win over others."
RX: Accept Everything; Relaxation

15.   "Life is serious business."
RX: Say "So What"; Do Nothing

CHANGING YOUR EXTERNAL LIFESTYLE (BEHAVIOR)

External changes in an obsessive-compulsive lifestyle are critical to healing. Making concrete changes in behavior as an expression of internal healing signifies growth and symbolizes commitment to healthy living. Take pride and reassurance in the changes made in our outward lifestyle. Concrete changes are something we can weigh and measure and hang onto in difficult times. When we have set a boundary regarding work hours and honor this boundary, a strong line of protection is created against compulsive tendencies.

The *danger* in making external changes for compulsive doers lies in losing touch with the power of being and getting lost in the action itself, thus creating more *doing* in the process! It is best to proceed slowly through the following recommendations. Be careful to take into account your inner pacing and rhythm. Compulsive doers are notorious for jumping into many projects at the same time, trying to do everything "perfectly", and then ending up as empty and unfulfilled as at the beginning. Don't let this happen to you on your journey to being.

As with the Internal Lifestyle changes, if these suggestions are not working, it is possible that additional therapeutic work around your family of origin needs to be done.

Another important point to re-emphasize is while compulsive doing *can* be abstained from, we *cannot* abstain from work itself. We must learn to live in harmony with the substance (work) of our "addiction". This makes it even more important to find methods that work in seeking to *balance* work and other aspects of life. *Balance for the compulsive doer is the same as abstention for the substance dependent person.*

Use the ODIST

While looking at ways to change external behaviors it may be helpful to look over the items you responded to positively on the "Over Doing It Screening Test". Looking at the specific items can give a sense for what areas of behavior are unhealthy and obsessive-compulsive. You may also want to ask others how they see you in regard to these items.

The ODIST was originally designed as a measure of compulsive doing tendencies. It can also be a very helpful guide in designing a balanced lifestyle. Each compulsive doer has certain areas that are particularly problematic. We all have areas of our life that are doing well. Recognizing problem areas helps to put recovery energies where they will do the most good.

Take Actual Time-Out From Work

I know. I said earlier that compulsive doers cannot totally avoid work. While that may be the case in the long run, some fortunate compulsive doers are in a financial position to take an extended leave of absence from the workplace itself. While this does not guarantee that the individual is not going to "find" work in other areas of life to fill the gap left by the absence of actual employment duties, a leave of absence can assist in getting recovery started.

Compulsive doers who are able and choose this intervention, report that their perspective on life and work changes. After two or three months without "legitimized" work with which to be distracted, the individual is often able to face and work through some of the issues underlying the work addictive process itself. *Rest itself is essential to the healing process.*

Learn to Say "NO"

This appears simple but is a very difficult principle to master. Compulsive doers have a great deal of trouble saying "No" to demands on time, resources, and energy. For most compulsive doers this is a result of fears of rejection and abandonment which run very deeply and are very powerful. Compulsive accomplishing covers over this fear. When saying "No" to people, guilt, anxiety and fear of abandonment is experienced.

Saying "No" does not always have to do with others' requests and demands. Often times our cruelest taskmaster is the doer within us. We drive ourselves to accomplish that last project, take care of that last errand, finish that last assignment. When we say "No" it often needs to be to *ourselves*. For example: "No, I will not run that last errand on the way to work. It's a sunny day and I would like to sit outside for a few minutes and enjoy the fresh air."

Saying "No" eventually means saying "Yes" to ourselves and our inner needs. It is also acknowledging fears around rejection, abandonment and co-dependency. This is not easy. Many struggle for years around this issue and still have a difficult time stopping the compulsion to give everyone what they want, to please everyone, and to make sure everyone is satisfied. We *can* do it though! We can say "No". We can start now and continue to practice. We can make friends with "No". Play with it, experiment and discover what feels like a good balance.

Be Willing To Give It Up

Yes, I'm afraid it's true! When "addicted" to anything we must be willing to give it up. If addicted to alcohol we need to be willing to stop drinking. If addicted to gambling, we need to be willing to stop gambling. When "addicted" to work, we need to be willing to stop *working*.

Being willing to give it up a need means that when family is asking for attention on Saturday afternoon (even though that report needs to be dictated for work, or the laundry finished, or the garage shelves rebuilt) we're willing to let go of that compulsion. When exercising if our body feels tired and ready to stop, be willing not to do that extra mile, or finish those final sit-ups. When at the office and it's time to leave for a support group meeting and we *really* want to finish the last page of that report, we need to be willing to let go of that, also.

Being willing to give it up means tuning in to that little voice (sometimes a *very* little voice!) inside warning when we are stepping over the line between productivity and addiction. We need to fine-tune this little voice, and learn its language, until we are able to listen to it continually and carefully. We need to rely on it to keep us in balance. This is not an easy task, particularly so in process compulsions where there is no external measurable substance which can tangibly be "put down" like a bottle, or pills.

It's very tempting to say "Yes" to shoulds even when we know that we're heading into unhealthy territory. It takes practice and courage to be willing to give up the craving for more work, accomplishing, and producing. We must develop this willingness if we are to recover health and serenity.

Use "I Statements"

In compulsive doing there is a strong tendency to control, caretake, project, and blame. We often feel it is the responsibility of the other person, or the situation that we are the way we are (See A Silent Day, Page 96). Compulsive doers have a tendency to even go so far as divorcing their spouse with the idea that their compulsive doing will clear up magically.

Compulsive doing is an *internal* process which only *we* can heal or change. It simply gets us more "stuck" to focus on the other person and what they are doing, even if what they are doing is not healthy. We need to stop externalizing our focus and bring it back within in order to get in touch with our power to *be*. A good way of doing this is through "I statements". When we make an "I statement" we are stating our feelings, thoughts, or needs. When we make a "you statement" we are projecting those needs, thoughts, or feelings onto the other person and become dependent on them to solve our problem, or provide for our needs.

When upset with your friend, spouse or children for "controlling" you or trying to change you or otherwise *doing* something to you, practice focusing instead on what you want to *be*. Ask, "Okay, maybe they are a bit dependent, or controlling, but what do

I want to be like now?" Perhaps the answer is that you wish to be able to assert your right to take some time to be by yourself. Perhaps you don't want to agree with everything the other person is saying on a subject. Let yourself take back the power to *be* who you want to be. Letting go of codependency will put you in a much better position to *be*.

Be Willing to Move

No, I'm not referring to moving to a new town in a country that has banished compulsive doing. Compulsive doers spend a great deal of time in their heads. We figure things out, plan ahead, mull things over, consider and deliberate, even develop mental constipation at times! When pursuing recovery from compulsive doing we have a tendency to get wrapped up in our thoughts also. The voices from our past tell us to "plan carefully", to not make "mistakes", to "think ahead". In our healing all this thinking can get us more caught up than ever.

Be willing to trust. Be willing to let go. Be willing to embrace change and disinhibit from forcing and shoulding. Being willing to move or to be active is the first step.

Acting means different things for different people at different times. Taking action can be attending a support group meeting even when afraid and uncomfortable. Acting can be letting go of obsessive, self-critical or controlling thoughts and going out dancing. Acting can be *expressing* emotions rather than being intellectual and "reasonable".

It may mean many other things, but it always means not obsessing, thinking or "staring" inside and wondering what is "wrong". When focusing inside obsessively, we lose touch with our energy, our bodies, our spontaneity. We need those qualities in our recovery. We need to move and feel the spontaneous energy in our physical bodies. We need to disinhibit and allow our feelings to flow.

Notice the next time you are thinking about what should be done, how you should be, or what the "right" path is for you at the moment. When you observe yourself engaged in such thoughts, look at what could be done to release some of your natural energy. Ask questions such as "How does my body feel right now?", or "What kind of energy do I have right now?". Then *act* on whatever response is received. This can be as simple as letting yourself tap your foot to music. It can be more involved like going roller skating or jogging. In any event, physical activity seems to assist in letting our natural energy out. When lost in thought, don't be afraid to *move*.

Pace Yourself

Everyone has a natural rhythm or energy flow. Compulsive doing separates us from that natural rhythm and locks us into *forcing* ourselves to do what we *should* do. We need to be empowered to find our own pace again.

One of the characteristic patterns is "getting things done" in a hurry. We focus on the outcome rather than the process and push to achieve that outcome whatever the cost in energy and time. What would it feel like to focus again on the *process.* How would it feel to enjoy each moment as it passes, rather that living so many days, weeks, or years ahead of ourselves? Examine the day today. What sort of qualitative difference would there be if you were pacing yourself with your natural energy flow? How would your choices be different? How would you feel about yourself and others? What needs and feelings would you be noticing that may not be there now?

In order to be paced, develop a sense for your own inner rhythm. To do this, stop your current activity and sit quietly for a few minutes, perhaps breathing deeply. It may be helpful to practice "centering" (see last section). Then ask, "Before I take my next action, I need to know if this action is coming from my natural energy, or from shoulds and forcing." Wait for an answer to arise from your own awareness. Continue asking this question as you move through the rest of the day. Be careful not to move too fast (e.g., doing two or three things at a time, or rushing from one thing to the next), or too slow (e.g., not doing anything and then getting so far behind there is a need to rush at the last minute). Instead, remain calm and aware of your inner rhythm.

Pacing is an excellent prevention for stress and fatigue. It also helps for awareness of feelings that our compulsive doing may cause us to ignore. Pacing helps us to feel mature, self-possessed and in balance. When we are pacing, we have a better opportunity to be in touch with what we want to do, be, and say.

Forcing and pacing are opposites that we need to be aware of in the process of recovery from compulsive doing.

Set Boundaries

A common topic in recent recovery literature (Beattie, 1987), boundaries are also essential to the process of healing from compulsive doing. Boundaries are those internal and external limits that we establish to protect ourselves from being over-run by other forces that are outside of our boundaries. Boundaries are our borders. Healthy boundaries are needed if we are to risk being vulnerable and intimate. Those raised in dysfunctional families often have had boundaries violated physically, emotionally, intellectually, or spiritually, or were never given guidance in establishing boundaries. This makes adult living rather challenging to say the least. There is no sense for what is "normal".

In recovery we need to set, reset and continually assess boundaries. Boundaries can come in many shapes, sizes, colors and forms. A boundary is set, for example, when choosing not to spend time with an obsessive-compulsive colleague. A boundary is set when we tell our spouse that help is needed with the housework and child care. A boundary is set when we say "No" to one more project or responsibility at the office. A boundary is set when we decide internally to not get dragged into an argument when our position has already been clearly stated. All are examples of setting boundaries around our needs. When we set boundaries we are saying that we will not let the other person, place, or circumstance go further with us. We are protecting our boundaries from others who are seeking to "act into" our life space.

Boundaries can also be set around our "acting out". This is especially important for compulsive doers tend to have problems with both "acting in" boundaries and with "acting out" boundaries. When setting acting out boundaries, put the reins on compulsive doing. For example, set a boundary to avoid completely overhauling the filing system at work since the old one is good enough. Set a boundary about not cleaning the house obsessively after every fight with your spouse or lover.

Often acting-out type boundaries are developed as a result of feedback from the environment. Friends or coworkers may finally sit us down and remind us that they are not robots designed to help us do more work. The friend we brush off at the grocery store because of overwork and being in a frenzy, may remind us that friendships need care and attention, too. Our bodies may "set boundaries" by letting us know, sometimes in painful ways, that we have been moving too fast and doing too much.

This feedback can be used to re-parent ourselves. Do-aholics often are not parented in healthy ways around work boundaries. We do not grow up with a sense of our limits and are baffled and hurt when the adult environment sets limits. It is good to listen to these messages and develop boundaries that will take care of our needs.

Set Limits

Limits are like boundaries except more external. A boundary is something set inside. A limit is something put out in the environment. We may decide not to take work out of the office, or to relegate it to one room in the house. We may set a limit on television watching so there is more time for our family. We may set limits on work hours so they will be more manageable. We may set a limit about not attending Saturday morning work meetings.

Make a list of limits and boundaries that you would like to set. You do not necessarily have to follow through with all of your ideas, but this exercise gives a sense of what works for you in these areas. Once you've made the list, check which items you'd like to take action on now and which ones to defer for later. Then go for it! Be alert as to how others react to your limits, or boundary setting. Also, notice how you feel about these changes. Often (like our addictions) our lack of limits and boundaries protects us from feelings that are uncomfortable or flat-out scary. Be open to what your feelings tell you as you attempt to set healthy boundaries and limits.

Design a Workable Schedule

Work schedules are clearly prescribed for some. For others, scheduling is left up to us. Much of this depends on the type of work we are involved in and the family demands in our life. Compulsive doers seem to do best with a clearly prescribed work schedule. Do-aholics are often more comfortable when they can "punch out" on the time clock at the beginning and end of the day. Such a routine gives automatic permission to relax and let go once free of the confines of the job. Of course, a true compulsive doer is likely to find ways to keep working even after they have punched out at their jobs! Often compulsive doers will even turn recreational activities or hobbies into money making hobbies. (Some even write books!)

Whether work hours are set or flexible, we need to have some sort of schedule to rely on. This is especially true in times of crisis when things are up in the air. Even during more placid days a schedule provides a path to balance for the obsessive-compulsive person.

As you work toward designing a personal schedule that works (and plays) for you, recall that compulsive doers cannot abstain permanently from work. Our addiction is carried within us and it's all around us in the environment. We cannot *not* work, but we *can* find a *balance*. Having a healthy schedule helps to find and maintain that balance.

One helpful visual image to use in setting a schedule is that of a pie. Cut up the pie into different sized portions depending on the activity. Examples of possible pie portions are job, spouse, children, friends, recreation, exercise, time alone, sleeping, unstructured time, eating, transportation, finances, shopping, etc. If 80 percent of our time goes to one area, such as work, only 20 percent is left to spend on all the other areas.

Go through each day of the week and design a careful schedule. Then get feedback on the schedule from someone who seems to have a well-balanced lifestyle and whom you respect. Then try out your schedule for a while and make alterations so that it's custom tailored just for you. Remember, human beings thrive on a basic routine. If there is a way to provide regularity in your sleep schedule, meal times, and work hours, do so! Also, remember the goal is not to "fit in" as much as possible, but rather to pace yourself and include a balance of needs, wants, and "must dos".

Set Your "Activity Zones"

Compulsive doers have difficulties in saying "No" to work and "Yes" to play. In order to reverse this we need to have a way to give ourselves permission to let go and play. One way to do this is through setting up "zones".

In order to set up personal activity zones, first define which hours of which days during the week (each day may be different) you work (red zones), which hours you *may* do work-type activities (yellow zones) and which times you will *play*, be, relax, and have fun (green zones).

When in a red zone, free youself from guilt about working. Although you do not allow yourself to get out of touch with pacing, feelings, and boundaries, realize that this is a time you need to do things that you may not necessarily want to do.

When in a yellow zone (it's probably wise to keep yellow zones to a minimum) answer business phone calls, do an odd load of laundry, or work on returning correspondence you may not be that excited about. You can also go out for a frozen yogurt, take a walk, or sit on the porch in the sun if desired. Here there's more of a blend of activities, some work and some fun.

In the green zone *only* play. Be completely focused on what you *want* to do, say, or be. Activities center around what makes you feel good about yourself. Green zones are where compulsive doers can really get a sense for the power of their compulsivity and how difficult it is to get permission to let go. Struggle to calm down even if feeling like a car that has its motor running a mile a minute in idle. Guilt, caretaking, and controlling urges may be overwhelming at times. Green zones are "work" for compulsive doers to establish! They are also very healing. If *working*, or unable to relax in the green zone time, this tells something very valuable about the need for more recovery work and self-permission-giving. People need to play. If we cannot play something needs adjusting.

Remember That Less Is More

Many people have been trained to think in terms of doing as much as possible in as little time as possible as quickly as possible. Success and progress is then measured in terms of how much is done with how little time. This notion is so deeply ingrained in our culture that it seems almost un-American to question it's validity. We *must*, however, if we are going to develop a healthier internal perspective on work as well as make healthy choices in behavior.

Examine your current life situation. Notice areas in which you have made an effort to "streamline" — only to find that you made room for more things you "need" to do. For example, you may now have a housekeeper who comes in to get done some of the chores for which you do not have time. What are you doing with that time that was saved? Do you spend that time relaxing and playing with the dog, or going for a walk with a friend? Do you use it to play a game with your children, or go to a movie, or maybe simply just sit and practice "being" on the couch?

What many tend to do is to fill that time with extra projects, business phone calls, non-essential errands, etc. This is because (as discussed in the previous Chapters) much compulsive work/doing behavior involves what is inside — the fears that drive us. Having less to do often has little to do with whether we do less!

Do not wait for all of those fears to be worked out in family of origin work. Make a conscious choice to use the time created for ourselves with microwave ovens and personal copiers to relax and play. Like most of these interventions this one takes practice and a certain degree of will-power. Feelings of guilt, or anxiety may come up as a result. That does not mean that we are not doing the right thing for ourselves. On the contrary, when it comes to compulsive doing — less is more.

If You Don't Use It You Won't Lose It

In conjunction with the less is more philosophy, it is also helpful to plan into the day a certain degree of "slop". Now, this doesn't mean sloppy slop, but rather little bits of time that can be "wasted". Often compulsive doers tend to take the straightest line between two points. Yet that may not be what we *feel* like doing! (Elsewhere in this section a technique called "Wandering" is discussed which, in part, is based on this idea.) We need to be able to listen to ourselves and maintain some sort of contact with what we *want* to be doing versus what we think we *should* be doing. In order to do this we need to learn not to crowd in so much stuff to do that we don't have any discretionary time.

During a normal day this means reminding yourself that it's okay to take the long route to work that would be enjoyed. It is also okay to linger at the copy machine collating a document which the machine could collate. It is also okay to walk to lunch rather than take a cab, or to take the stairs rather than the elevator.

While there may be a fear that something terrible is going to happen if we don't do things in the most direct and efficient way possible, this is not the reality. You will not lose it if you don't use it! Rather you will gradually learn to have more of an inner sense of self and of your own rhythms and needs. Life is not just about getting things done, but about enjoying the process. As the saying goes, "There is more to life than increasing its speed."

Making Do

Let's face it! We do not need as much as we have. Many people complain about the hectic nature of life and yet seem to feel the need to grab onto every opportunity that comes along. It can be very healing to realize that we do not need to do it all, even when we can.

Many people report feeling that their lives are too complex. It is important to realize that there is something to *do* about that. When we are considering buying a new car which will require working extra hours to pay for it, stop and ask if this is *really* what makes happiness. Do you really *want* a new car, or are you *really* interested in having more time to go for a relaxing drive in the country with your spouse?

Life is manageable to the degree that the choices that are made are consistent with the needs we have. If we listen to the messages in the media and society, we are likely to become lost, confused, overloaded, and more of a reflection of someone else's needs than our own. Some of the happiest and most fulfilled people are those who have made a conscious effort to lead very simple lives. We can do more with less and we do not have to do, or possess everything that is available to us!

Look Where You Are Going

There is a saying in Eastern countries that "If you don't change your direction, you are likely to end up where you are headed." I like to say "Look where you are going, or you may run into something you don't want to". As a psychologist, I have many opportunities to speak to groups of people on different topics. If I took advantage of every one of these opportunities I would quickly become very popular, but also totally exhausted. Opportunities are everywhere in today's society. There are challenges galore all around us. That does not mean that we have to accept all of those challenges, or that something is wrong with us if we do not! We can use boundary setting skills to say "No".

It is helpful for people to develop a sense for what direction they are headed in life. It just makes sense to know what is important and what is not. Do you value family, church activities, physical exercise, career? When you know what you *really* want, you can direct your energies appropriately and make choices that are consistent with those needs and goals.

Often there is too much emphasis on things (usually work-related) that are not in a personal "master-plan" for living. When noticing that this is happening (or has happened, as is more often the case), choose to let go of these projects and activities that are not assisting in getting you where you want to go.

This is best done as a actual paper and pencil task. Take a few minutes and write down your short term and long term goals in life. Then put the list away and think about it for a week, or so. Now go back and review the list making any changes you feel are appropriate.   Next make another list of the amount of time that you spend each week on different areas of your life such as family, spouse, exercise, play, work, house cleaning, etc.   Look at the kinds of projects and activities that you take on and what areas occupy most of your energy.   Finally, combine the two lists together.   If they match up, great.   If they do not, you have some changes to make in how you spend your time.

Listen To Your Body

Our bodies give continual messages about what is healthiest in each moment of the day.   For example people can frequently sense what type of food they need to be eating just as easily as they know when they are thirsty.   Our bodies tell when they are tired and when they are perky.   They tell when we are anxious and when we are relaxed.   They also tell when and what type of work is healthy for us.

If you are the most outgoing in the middle to late afternoon, it does not make sense to schedule an important meeting, class, or workshop in the early morning.   If you feel exhausted and drained by teaching a class at night, it might be much better holding it in the morning hours when fresh.

It is important to listen to the rhythms of the physical body.   When we don't, we end up *forcing* ourself to do things that are not right for us.   That brings us further away from an inner choiceful self and leads to a should-based lifestyle.   That in turn leads to greater and greater amounts of work.   ("Why not work if I'm not feeling alive anyway?" we might ask.)   What is needed is more aliveness and that comes through acceptance, not denial, of self and needs.

Speed Kills

When the phrase "speed kills" was first coined it was a warning about the dangers of drug abuse. Here it is used in a similar sense as a caution about the dangers of moving too fast through life. Workaholics are famous for doing a lot of stuff fast.   That is because the focus is on the goal and not the process.

When we notice that we are moving quickly it is a sign that something is wrong — that we have, in some way, fallen back into shoulds and lost touch with what we want. Sometimes the environment really does demand quick reactions, but this is actually much less common than thought.   More often, we start moving quickly because we are running away from something such as feelings, rather than *towards* something. It can also suggest that we have gotten lost in our goals.   Knowing this, pay attention to the pace and notice when trying to do two things at once, or rushing from the car to the office, or pushing to get through a project.

When this is happening, choose to stop and listen to the inner voice again. Ask, "Do I really need to get this done so fast, or am I pushing myself because: I feel guilty; I'm afraid to relate to people; I'm afraid of _____; I'm addicted to stress; etc.?" The answer to that question will tell much about what makes you tick and will also assist in slowing down. Remember, speed kills spontaneity and aliveness!

Take Vacations

A vacation is a great big "green zone". (See Page 143) For compulsive doers vacations can be frightening. While others look forward to vacations, compulsive doers sometimes come to dread the process of getting ready to leave, getting things in order after returning, and especially the feelings of guilt and lack of direction that come up during the trip. If we remember that compulsive doing is about a denial of painful and scary feelings, it's no surprise that being without work can be overwhelming. Going on vacation for the workaholic is like going cold turkey from a favored substance being abused. Both on a physical and an emotional level much upset and inner turmoil can be experienced.

This does not mean that vacations, like green zones, are not healthy and healing for compulsive doers, just that they are not always smooth and easy. There are some things to help deal with vacation time in a positive manner. First of all, it is important to avoid getting trapped into vacation plans for which you do not feel ownership. Compulsive doers fear loss of identity. Have some say in the travel plans. If traveling with someone else, make it a 50/50 enterprise and make sure to get your feelings heard.

Second, it's important to plan ahead. Plan the vacation times during "low" periods of the year when compulsive doing is likely to be at its worst. In

Northern climates this means February through April, but this may not necessarily be the same for you. Go with what works. Also, go to the place that works for you. Many compulsive doers will try to schedule a ton of sightseeing on vacation to feel they have "accomplished" something. Realize that a vacation is not designed to accomplish, but to relish! Remember too that it is important to allow enough time to decelerate from your compulsive doing. Going away for only a weekend can be more stressful for some compulsive doers than staying home and gardening or reading a good book. If you cannot get away for a reasonable length of time then make sure there will be plenty of time to *be* where you are going.

Third, once at your vacation destination it may be helpful to set up routines. While not wanting to act out compulsive doing in the vacation environment, avoid frightening yourself with the prospect of endless days with nothing to do. (For many compulsive doers this is similar to forcing a person who is phobic about elevators to ride up and down the Sears Tower in Chicago!) What to look for is a balance. For example, you might like to schedule a swim or a run first thing in the morning to feel that something was accomplished right off the bat. That may assist in letting go later and feeling less guilt about indulging in play and relaxation.

Finally, it is never helpful to bring work along on vacation! If you are not around work activities there is no way to *do* them! Being on vacation is "work" enough for compulsive doers. There a chance to practice letting go and being kind to ourselves.

Practice saying "no" to the guilt and drivenness and forcing of yourself to accomplish things. Looking at a vacation as a chance to heal yourself in your mind as well as your body sheds a new light on this important part of life.

Wander

No, this is not a new type of break dance! Wandering is a concept developed in working with compulsive doers that assists in breaking the addictive cycle of shoulding and accomplishing.

In order to "wander" set aside a period of time (a couple of hours should do fine) such as a lunch time or a Saturday afternoon. Then set out on foot, walking, running, on a bike, in a car, or whatever suits your current mood and circumstances. Next just ask yourself where you would like to go *now*. Keep in mind that during this period of time there is no *reason* to go anywhere in particular. If you think "Gee, I could stop at the hardware store and pick up those light bulbs we need," simply redirect your attention away from that should and back to where you *want* to be heading.

This may sound like a silly thing to do, but for compulsive doers it is a very powerful intervention! Wandering is a process of rediscovery of yourself. Wandering lets you listen to your own urges and impulses. It allows a time to get back into your spontaneous self that seems so distant when acting out compulsive doing.

All compulsive doers should wander at least one time every week at a minimum. If you can do it more and feel comfortable with that, so much the better! Think of wandering as a pilgrimage to find your spontaneous self to get back in touch with your *power of being.*

Own Your Lists

For many people lists are a wonderful invention. Lists can help people to get organized and to balance their time and activities. For compulsive doers lists can be instruments of terrorism! Compulsive doers sometimes come into my office clutching their lists, unable to let them out of their sight. (In fact, compulsive doers have refused to let me see their lists or to leave them in my office while in the restroom!)

List-making is about not trusting. When we do not trust ourselves, our destiny or our God to get done what needs to be done, we make lists to try to *control* life. Then we are hurt or confused when life does not conform to the lists. We get frustrated and furious at people, events, and circumstances that get in the way of the "completion" of the lists. We wake up in the middle of the night writing down more "to dos" for ourselves. We pray to our list-god in the morning before leaving the house. We get in fender-benders driving around reading our lists.

Trust in yourself. Unless you have a brain injury, you will be able to get done what needs to be done for life to work out. List-making only gets you more *objectified* and farther from spontaneous reactions.

If you have a list now try this experiment. Put the list at the bottom of a drawer. Then go about daily life for 48 hours or so. Now go back and check the list. Chances are the important things on the list got done anyway, right?

One last comment on lists and list making. I do not mean to give the impression that lists are inherently bad. This is no more true than to say that work itself is inherently negative. This is simply not true. As with alcohol, what is important is how you USE your lists. Do you let it control you, or do you own it? When we are clear that lists are an expression of our choices for living, they can be a great help. When we fall into treating lists as manifestations of internal shoulds they serve to amplify those very shoulds and give them more power over us. Lists are fine, if they are choiceful expressions of our power of being.

Let Go of Measures

As humans we have a tendency to want to measure, calibrate, assess, count, weigh and categorize. As with list making, measuring things is fine — if done for healthy reasons. Society would become rather unmanageable if we could not measure things. On the other hand, measuring things can quickly take on a very compulsive quality that externalizes our focus in life.

Time is a good, ever present example of the importance of how we treat our measurements. In general, societies further from the equator tend to have a more rigid sense of time and to lend more importance to it's measurement. Societies closer to the equator often take a more relaxed approach to time. Time measuring devices such as the watches that most wear, were developed by time-conscious people in more northerly climates.

The point is there is no one way of dealing with time. All people experience the passage of time in some way or another, but those experiences vary greatly. I had a very up-tight professor once who made a big issue of the importance of students being exactly on time for class. This meant not one second late! On a recent trip to Hawaii I found that even banks and government buildings did not necessarily open even close to the scheduled time. It is okay to consciously decide how to relate to time and other forms of measurement in the world.

Try this experiment next time there is a day off from work. Take your watch off and leave it next to bed at night. Then go without a watch throughout the day off. Stay conscious of how this effects your feelings about time. Notice if any feelings of fear, guilt, or need to control arise. (For many people letting go of measuring devices is comparable to a drug addict letting go of his or her drug of choice.) Realize that nowhere is it decreed that you have to be controlled by time.

Do One Thing at a Time

This is a big one for compulsive doers. Most work addicts *know* what I am talking about. You know what it's like to comb your hair, brush your teeth and put on deodorant at the same time. You've watched yourself eating lunch, talking on the phone and reading a report while waiting for your secretary to give the information you requested. You know how easy it becomes to take care of a scheduling problem on the cellular phone while driving to an appointment and checking your notes ahead of time.

Doing more than one thing at a time is one of the major indicators of compulsive doing. Look at your life closely. Pretend a parrot is on your shoulder as you go through the day. "Braak... watch what you're doing, watch what you're doing!" is a reminder to yourself as you eat breakfast while ironing clothes. "Squaak...one thing at a time; one thing at a time," chirp to yourself while juggling the groceries, balancing the checkbook and mentally reviewing a shopping list. In this way it's possible to learn to let go of doing more than one thing and begin to find more pleasure in the thing that is being done.

When people do several things at once it is usually out of a sense of guilt, over-responsibility, or fear of "messing up" and being rejected. When you allow yourself to do what you are doing and have that be enough, you honor yourself and make the statement "I am good enough. I have a right to exist!"

Stop Doing it All

Fears of abandonment and rejection come into play in an obsessive-compulsive desire to "do it all". Just as we attempt to be perfect, we also like to imagine we can do it all. With lists in hand, we charge out into the day ready to do battle with all things incomplete and unpolished. We fix, repair, change, alter, create, innovate and renovate until reaching some arbitrary limit set in our heads. The trouble is, by the time we accomplish all we "want" to, there is little or no time for *us*!

We may even hear the comment from others that we are "selfish", that we only see our own needs, projects, and itineraries. While it may appear that the compulsive doer is singlemindedly pursuing what they "want" to do, actually what happens is closer to enslavement. Do-aholics become slaves to accomplishment and fear dire consequences when they cannot.

Moving through the day, it's important to remind yourself you do *not* have to get everything done. Let yourself off the hook. learn to delegate tasks and projects. Let go of things which you do not *have* to do and do not want to do. Allow yourself to feel the guilt and the fear of rejection that come up naturally as you put down your lists and acknowledge your limitations. Gradually you discover that you are okay without all of the accomplishing and pushing of yourself. Later, you will even begin to be comfortable with the feelings that arise when you are not overworking yourself.

Act "Irresponsibly"

This is one of my personal favorites! Acting irresponsibly goes along well with the technique of saying "So what" (from the last section of this chapter). Our society teaches in many ways to "grow up" and to "be responsible". Frivolity, adventurism and childishness are shunned by "wise" elders. And so we learn to be good grown-ups grimly going through our paces. For many of us, even play takes on the seriousness of competition. We "work hard and play hard" as if the two were the same thing. While some people are able to keep a sensible balance in their lives, compulsive doers tend to be relentlessly driven.

Yuck! Life should be more than all that serious stuff. Inside each of us is a child who delights in spontaneity and impulsivity. This inner child can be released by avoiding our usual overly responsible self-talk. Give yourself permission to be irresponsible — whatever that means for you. Remind yourself that the "responsible" voice inside most likely is a reflection of an unhealthy parent who didn't know any more about living than you do and probably didn't have much fun anyway. It's up to you what people will say about you in your epitaph, "She had fun and sometimes got silly", or "She gave her life to further the cause of seriousness".

Own Yourself in Relationships

Compulsive doers have strong tendencies toward control and caretaking. These tendencies can get us into trouble in relationships, particularly those that are most intimate. We need to be able to maintain a sense of self-ownership and self-responsibility, both when alone and when we are functioning in relationships with others.

As mentioned earlier, one of the best techniques for doing this is by making "I statements". They deserve further mention here. "I statements" help to own our own feelings, as opposed to "you statements" which tend to project feelings unto others around us. When using an "I statement" you state your need, feeling, or idea clearly to the other person. "I statements" often sound like the following: "When you _____ I feel _____ and I would like it if you would _____".

Sound simple? Well, think about how often you've felt yourself getting more and more focused on *the other person* to whom you are relating. Your statement may have sounded something like, "You're so controlling. All you want to do is make me into your mother." We lose our focus on our our needs (See last section) and extend our control outside of ourselves to try and "fix" or change the other person.

Changing other people doesn't work. What to do instead is focus on yourself. In the previous example instead say, "I feel unwilling to go along with what you are asking. I am wondering if there is more to your request than you have shared with me?" This type of "I statement" brings you naturally and effortlessly back to an awareness of *your* needs, opinions, and feelings. Become responsible for yourself and in so doing gain increased flexibility and freedom. You are no longer locked into fixing or changing the other person and can make decisions more clearly about how to take good care of yourself.

"I statements" also remind you that you are 100 percent responsible for only one thing in life — yourself! That is all that can be controlled and all that can be changed. Until that is realized, a great deal of energy is wasted and you feel frustrated, confused and often victimized by others. Remind yourself that relationships are never 50/50; they are always 100/100. When you own yourself 100 percent, you begin to grow and become more effective as a person, a partner, a parent and a friend.

Start Slowly in the Morning

How often do compulsive doers begin the day in a whirlwind of activity and effort? No sooner does the alarm go off and we are running from task to task getting ready for the day and fitting in a few "extra" projects here and there before going to work. (Like replastering the bathroom or cleaning out all the closets!)

How the day is started has a big effect on what happens *during* the day. Early morning activity sets the tone for the activity level later on. Compulsive doers in particular need to begin the day in a peaceful, accepting, and placid manner. Then that mood can be carried with us as we pace ourselves through the day. This is something that requires *practice*. It doesn't come easily and you will have to keep reminding yourself to "slow down" and "take it easy"!

It is helpful for compulsive doers to spend at least five to ten minutes just laying in bed upon awakening. As you lay there do a "status check" on your body. Do you have any particular sore spots or tension? Are you still tired or rested? What is happening for you *emotionally*? Do you feel healthy or sickly? Are you tense and anxious? Is you mind racing a mile a minute? About what? Once you have a sense for how you are doing, appropriate action can be taken. If you are tired, don't push it. Take it especially easy today. If you are sore or tense physically, do some stretching while still in bed. If you are experiencing an emotion, try to identify it and give yourself permission to feel the feeling, or even do some journaling about it. The important thing is to become aware of how you feel and to act in accordance with that, rather than forcing yourself into doing and shoulding right away. This way your early morning time can set a healthy pace for the rest of your day.

Lay it Down Before Lying Down

The way in which the day is ended is just as important as the way in which it is begun. Many compulsive doers complain about having difficulty falling asleep, staying asleep, and waking up (either too early or too late!). Much of this has to do with the compulsive doers' tendency to worry over things done or not done the day before, or what will happen in the day to come.

It is helpful for compulsive doers to keep a journal. This assists in working through feelings and facilitates the inner growth process. This journal can be placed next to the bed where it will be easily accessible. Before you settle down for the night, take a few minutes to make a list of all the things on your mind at the time. After you write them down, close your journal and *let them go*. If you find yourself returning to them, remind yourself that they are written down and you can deal with them in the morning. This frees you to let go and embrace sleep with a relaxed mind.

"Fake It Till You Make It"

Sometimes we are feeling inhibited. Sometimes we feel like work is everything. Sometimes we are uptight, tense and emotionally constricted. Those are the times that we need to be willing to stretch out a little. When we don't *feel* relaxed and open we can still *act* that way.

Sometimes all that is needed to begin feeling more spontaneous is to act more that way for a while. Soon the "act" awakens the real spontaneity within and you come alive. "Fake it till you make it". Disinhibit because that is what you want. The *patterns* are there waiting to be awakened within. Encourage yourself to relax by acting that way and then allowing your inner self to catch on. Go through the motions and soon you will *be* in motion. Go dancing, play with the dog, play a game of tennis. Do whatever it is that works for you. Pry loose from shoulding and forcing by acting a bit irreverent and playful.

Develop Multiple and Varied Supports

During the journey of recovery from compulsive doing, there are many different types of people and relationships around us. Some people may be very close like our children, spouse, or lover. Some people may be more peripheral. Some may be active compulsive doers. Others may have healthy lifestyle attitudes.

During compulsive times we tend to become isolated in working, striving, and accomplishing. In healing times, we benefit from *being* around others (Wotitz, 1990). Healthy role models can be found. Feelings are shared and worked through. Support and encouragement are received. Acceptance and love for who we are is available. All of these things come from others.

For compulsive doers, the task of connecting with others involves slowing down enough to *see* them and slowing down enough to *show* them yourself. To the degree that compulsive doing is about the fear of rejection (or conversely, the loss of identity) you will instinctively avoid others. When the pace is slowed down, it's like suddenly finding yourself in the same "dimension" as others. Sharing your fears about this can help a great deal.

It is healthy to have relationships and to want relationships in life. It is healthy to have multiple relationships to avoid a crisis with "all relationship eggs in one basket". It is healthy to have close relationships where the risk has been taken to expose feelings and show fear of rejection and of not being perfect. These relationships will then be there to assist in the healing process.

To get connected with others, first slow down, then get centered in who *you* are as a person. Next risk sharing through "I statements" and owning feelings honestly. Finally, there is the need to trust and detach to avoid attempts to caretake and control the other person. (Notice that internal knowing and loving comes *before* reaching out to others.) Slowly, over time the network of friendships and intimacies is built that are needed for inner healing and outer stability.

Give Yourself Permission to be Alone

As important as others are to the healing process, so is being alone. Many people (about one third of the general population) are natural "introverts". Society and its compulsive doing lifestyle, are often very "extroverted". This makes it critical to allow time to be alone each week, even each day if that is what is needed. As always, balance is the key. Spending all available time alone is not healthy. Spending all of it with others isn't healthy either.

It is helpful to designate a few specific times during the week to be *really* alone. This is a time when there is no need to be in a "role" for anyone such as parent, teacher, faithful employee. You can just be yourself. I still like to go for a drive into the country and sit on the hood of my car for a while. I have noticed that it is helpful for me to physically get away from those environments where my role demands are strong such as at work or at home. It helps to combine time alone with other techniques such as "wandering", or "doing nothing" to assist in re-connecting with ourselves.

Practice Active Relaxation Methods

There are a wide variety of techniques which have been developed to assist in developing a psychophysiological relaxation response (David, et al 1982). Compulsive doers *need* to practice active relaxation methods. Because practicing abstinence doesn't mean totally avoiding work, it is important to achieve a state of balance between doing and being. Relaxation techniques assist in doing this.

One of the most powerful, healthy and easy to use relaxation techniques is simply breathing! Our breath has a powerful influence on us and the manner of breathing (eg., tense shallow breaths versus relaxed full breaths) says a great deal about our internal state at the time. For centuries different philosophies and religions have espoused the benefits of healthy breathing and breath control. It is no coincidence that many athletes also focus so much attention in this area.

One breathing technique that is helpful for compulsive doers is called Misogi Breathing (Tohei, 1978, Crum, 1987). Misogi breathing arises from the Japanese martial arts where it is used in developing the balanced and centered state necessary to perform martial art techniques. In order to do Misogi

Breathing simply begin breathing through your nose, deep into your throat, and then exhale through your mouth making a "haaa" sound as you do so. The trick is to breathe down into your stomach so that your abdomen expands rather than your upper chest. Imagine your breath getting deeper and fuller, cascading like waves on a shore, radiating healing energy outward from your stomach area to your entire body, slowly filling you with relaxation and healing energy. See your inhalations and exhalations as a circle. Breathe in healing energy and exhale tensions, control, forcing, frustration and any other unhealthy compulsive doing by-products sensed within you at the time. Then feel the healing and relaxing energy filling the space that is left.

Misogi breathing, like other active relaxation methods, can really be practiced anywhere and at any time while stressed. It can be used as an intervention at times when compulsive doing is becoming overpowering, or just as a way to take a break and get back on track.

Another active relaxation strategy that is helpful for compulsive doers is developing "cues" and "signals" in the environment as reminders to relax (e.g., do Misogi breathing, etc.). For example, some people purchase a package of colored dots with adhesive on the back from an office supply store. These dots can be placed in strategic locations around the home, office, even on the rear view mirror of your car. When you see the dot it is a reminder to relax, slow down, and pace yourself. The more time allowed to "honor" the dot and let it serve as a trigger for your

relaxation response, the more powerful an effect it
will have.

Because of the wide variety of relaxation methods
available, it helps to purchase your own workbook in
this area. You can then select which techniques work
best for you. The *Relaxation and Stress Reduction
Workbook* (1982) is an excellent resource in this area.

Make Your Work and Living Space Relaxing

Compulsive doers spend a great deal of time
working. It is surprising, therefore, that more
attention is not given to making our work space and
our home comfortable. If you have an office or other
designated work space, take some time out from the
activities you *do* there and think about how you
would like that space to *be*. Would some plants be
enjoyable? Would some pictures hanging nearby be
helpful? Would a coat-hook on the back of the door
be a nice convenience? "Brainstorm" a list of ideas
including the most wild and impractical ones. Weed
out those that won't do and select those that really
will do. Invest the time to make them happen. Then
relax and enjoy your new "oasis".

Work "Smart" Not "Hard"

Compulsive doers usually like to do everything
possible and to do it all alone. Caretaking and
controlling instincts lead to obsessiveness about
getting everything possible, and even impossible, done
and without the assistance of others. Often our idea
of "teamwork" and delegating is to draw others into

our work frenzy and use them as extensions of our controlling in order to get more done.

Working "smart" involves establishing work behaviors that enhance the ability for self care and for pacing in work situations. Working smart includes taking minute breaks. Delegate to others and then *let go* of what was delegated and trust the abilities of the other party. Scheduling work to fit with personal highs and lows during the day. Learn to work as a team with others. Surrender the need to control everything. Invest time and energy in an effective approach rather than the more traditional "shotgun" approach characteristic of compulsive doers.

Set a "Relaxation Boundary"

Many compulsive doers who work outside the home find it helpful to set up a "relaxation boundary" between work and home. This transition zone provides time to unwind and relax before actually arriving home. This way, any compulsive energy that may have been generated during the work period can be dissipated rather than dumped into the home.

One example of such a transitional activity is stopping at the health club to exercise. Another is purchasing a newspaper and pausing for 15 minutes at a park to read. Still another is finding a support group meeting to attend immediately after work. The idea is to choose something that fits, that won't take up too much time, but serves as an actual (or even symbolic) transition from the "red" work zone to the "green" home zone.

Love Someone

Someone once said that to really love someone you need to first accept them for who they are and then accept them for who they are not! Compulsive doers are tempted to control, change, fix, or do anything *but* accept others. This is especially true in the closest relationships with spouses and significant others in particular.

A wonderful thing happens when we are really able to let go and *see* someone for just who they are. By accepting another person, we in turn get permission for self acceptance. This is a terrific feeling for someone used to the emptiness of controlling and caretaking others in relationships.

To practice this principle, be willing to let go of the idea that feelings are dependent on the other person's behavior and that it is possible to change the other person in any way. When you let go, the feelings of aliveness and acceptance will begin to filter in. In turn these feelings will lead back to your own power of being.

Develop A Power of Being Community

We need to have other people around who are part of a community that values the power of being. It is important to share feelings openly with others who can be trusted and who are accepting us without trying to "fix" or change us. More support is needed than just once-weekly therapy sessions or reading self-help books. We need to be "exposed" emotionally.

We need to know that we are not alone. We need to create a healthy family system(s) to replace the one not available as children. We need a sense of self-worth and of hope for continued healing. We need to have others behaving in healthy ways and taking good care of themselves as models. We need to let go or surrender to a group while maintaining a healthy sense of boundaries. We also need people on which to project unmet childhood needs and feelings and then discover the ability to own and work through these feelings.

All of this can be found at 12-step meetings and other support groups, or in a group of selected friends. Compulsive doers on the road to the power of being would benefit from attending one or two group meetings each week. Although there are a wide variety of self-help groups available, those most useful for compulsive doers appear to be Workaholics Anonymous, Adult Children of Alcoholics, Alanon, and Co-Dependents Anonymous. All of these Anonymous groups use the 12-step format originally designed by Alcoholics Anonymous. (A.A. has the highest known success rate in helping people to recover from compulsive behavior.)

Your local newspaper, phone book, or community mental health center are resources for locating self-help groups. After "tapping into" one group you will probably hear about others. Don't be afraid to experiment with different groups. Trust your *feelings* to tell what is right for you at this time. Later, as you move along in your growth process another type of group may be more helpful. Most groups have few membership requirements and only accept free-will donations.

Another helpful resource is the *Recovery Resource Guide* by Robert Ackerman, Ph.D. and Judith A. Michaels, M.A. This inexpensive book gives a very complete overview of organizations, books, pamphlets, audio cassettes, etc. A therapist may also be able to recommend groups that will be helpful for your healing journey.

Ultimately, a growing sense of the power of being leads to the creation of your own community. This journey is likely to lead to contact with like spirited fellow travelers. Also, luck may bring folks who are further along the path and can act as guides, models, or coaches. It is wise to avoid squandering these important relationships. A connection is awakened when your own journey towards being is shared with fellow travelers. This is probably the most difficult quest that anyone goes on in their life and all the camaraderie available is needed.

You Can Take it With You!

Recovery from compulsive doing is an ongoing, exciting, and challenging process. Carry the healing process wherever you go. Bring this, or another favorite book along during travels. When some encouragement, support, suggestions or clarification is needed, take a few minutes to read a passage that hits home. Give yourself permission to use resources to make your personal journey easier. If nothing else, having a resource along provides a reminder that the quest is not done alone in the move from doing to being.

I want to re-emphasize that ALL of the suggestions for internal and external growth and change take PRACTICE! This is very, very difficult work. It is good to be thankful even for little gains that are made towards the power of being. Remember, the first time anything new is tried, it's common to feel less than adequate and have minimal results. This does NOT mean that the wrong thing is being done. All it means is keep practicing. Eventually the power of being CAN be recovered, but it's misleading to believe the road is not long and at times difficult. Keep moving forward and focusing on what is wanted rather than what is not wanted and the way will be found.

Finally, Appendix B contains a list of "Some Stress Management Tools for Compulsive Doers". This list gives additional brief suggestions for external behavior changes that are healing and healthy. As with all of the suggestions in this book, use what works and leave the rest for someone else. You may also want to spend time writing down your own ideas for interventions that would be helpful in your life. Each of us must travel a unique path. No two compulsive doers are the same, nor are the same things needed to get healthy again.

Now, imagine for a minute that a great deal of the past three chapters of this book has been put into practice in your daily life. What would life look like? What kind of choices would you make? How would it *feel* and how would you *act* if you were well into the healing process and the power of being had grown strong within?   The next chapter is designed to provide insights into the lifestyle changes available through recovery from compulsive doing and what can be expected in your own life as the path back to your natural self is followed.

ONCE A FOREST

Wipe away your sleepy tear
And come in close to hear
This may be the last stop to where
I care to remember
Wide open wide
We were
I'm not sure why
Come sit beside the fire
It burns and it's
Life that's going by

One holds the light
One tells the story
Once we were ripe
Ripe and unfolding
But in the middle of the path
Laid bare before us
Once was alive
Once was a forest

While there's time
And there's breath left
Where we only reap
Before the whole wide world
Is undressed
Into nothing
Swept up in this forward motion
Rushing on
Like the first kiss
First words spoken
Here and gone

Elly Brown
from *Where We Live*, Copyright 1989, 1990

CHAPTER SEVEN: *"THE LIGHTHOUSE WITHIN"*

PATTERNS FOR LIVING IN THE POWER OF BEING

A s this chapter begins, I am sitting outside under a dusky sky with a magical moon on the rise. Leaves are blowing in the trees overhead and a fresh smell of spring is in the air. The community around me is alive with the voices of birds and children. The world seems incredibly beautiful in this moment. Everywhere I see gifts of experience to be unwrapped and lived. I am, for the present, in a state of *being*.

Life is *designed* to be indescribably wonderful in its essence. Just the basics of being alive (eating, breathing, working, sleeping) can be incredible experiences. We do not need to go out in search of stimulation and satisfaction, all that is needed is *right here* at each moment. The problem is not the way that LIFE is set up. The problem lies in how WE have been set up. It is as if God has created an amazingly beautiful symphony and the job is to construct (or, more accurately, discover) a receiver through which we are able to fully perceive the range and depth of that music. We *are* the receiver. The beautiful music is out there and has always been. The only question is if we are able to tune in to it.

Some of us are very damaged receivers. Compulsive doers, in particular, tend to rush so quickly through life that the music is missed, or only a vague background noise is heard. For the reasons discussed earlier in this book, letting life in is not easy. No matter how much we may be struggling, however, it is essential to keep in mind that right here and now (even as this is read) there are wonderful feelings and experiences all around. In that sense, there is *always* hope for rebirth and renewal in every moment of life.

All of us have moments, however brief, when the delicious beingness of life becomes obvious. Most wish that we could spend much more time feeling that peaceful sense of acceptance and aliveness that comes when life is in balance. The journey towards the *power of being* described in this book aims to increase and deepen this experience. While no one seems able to continually maintain this state of being, through dedicated attention to the principles discussed in this book, the path toward an ever-increasing quality of being can be found.

The potential we have as humans is amazing. The courage needed in order to realize that potential is equally incredible. Many are overcome by fear and refuse to call to adventure before they have even begun. Once the voyage is begun, the road to *being* leads through dark terrifying forests, barren lonely deserts, and hurricane-tossed seas. Many begin the journey and then stop at one stage or another. Still more become trapped in the confusion and paradox that lie as gate keepers to self-knowledge. Others are unable to make it back from the voyage and become lost out on the open uncharted sea.

The journey that awaits and surrounds is difficult, but one step leads to another and then another. We do not need to do more than we can do right now today. Life itself is *about* growth, discovery, and actualization. Gradually, as they arise, we will work through feelings and family of origin issues, develop skills for healthy external and internal living, and build a supportive community. We *can* heal ourselves in all of these ways, even simultaneously if we choose.

The purpose of this chapter is to look more closely at what it *feels* like to really live in the *power of being*. We know that the healing process will be difficult, but what kind of lifestyle is characteristic of compulsive doers who have the courage to traverse the path toward inner health? What will *we* be like when we have progressed along the healing path?

What will life look like? How will our goals, desires, and needs be altered by the healing process? As we have seen, compulsive doers, are likely to have parents that were compulsive in some form themselves. To make matters worse, the social context is one where compulsive doing is not only welcomed, but fostered and encouraged. Where, then, are role models? How do we know if we are on the right path? How do we measure progress and levels of health?

Obviously the answers to these questions are going to be different for each recovering compulsive doer. Each person's obsessive-compulsive traits will be very different from the next and needs for the healing process will be different also. Each of us needs to find our own way in the healing process. Some of the ideas and suggestions presented in this book will be helpful for you, others will not. Only by listening to the *inner voice* will you know what is right.

Remember, also how unhealthy it can be to look outside for how we "should" be healing. Should messages and the feeling of living for outside approval play a big part in setting us up for compulsive doing in the first place. One thing to be careful of even in reading a book such as this, is to remember that the answers are *inside*. What has been happening (hopefully) as you have been reading this book is that you have *rediscovered* some things that you already knew deep inside. Recovery from compulsive doing is about finding your identity *again*, not taking on an external model for what you should be like.

Words and ideas cannot really capture the *feeling* of being. There is no way to *know* what it is really like to be in touch with your spontaneous self except by *direct experience*. You will know what it is like to *be* when you have been there and not a minute before that! Most people recognize the spontaneous sense of aliveness that is characteristic of being and slowly begin to learn the individual psychological path they must follow to return again and again. Just as we develop the ability to walk, not from being told how, or "figuring it out," but by actual trial and error, so do we gradually develop an inner *experience* of what it is like to *be*. Gradually the awareness of the being side of living grows stronger and life without beingness begins to look flat and unfulfilling.

As healing from compulsive tendencies occurs, our perception of, and relationship to, the world begins to change in many ways. One of the most important changes seen is that we will, in fact, *do* less. More accurately, we will *do* less and *be* more! This is a very subtle and yet powerful shift that occurs for recovering compulsive doers.

A review of the world's literature in the area of religious and spiritual exploration reveals numerous references to this aspect of the *power of being*. For example, when one is on a spiritual journey in most religious or spiritual disciplines one is likely to spend a groat deal of time in prayer, meditation, or silent contemplation. People have consistently seemed to be best able to find themselves and their connection to their higher power through remaining still and simplifying life rather than being active and acting out. They have, in short, refocused themselves on the power of *being*.   People who are healing from compulsive doing will spend more time honoring that need to be still and listen to themselves.

Among the exercises suggested in Chapter Six, two of the most powerful for getting in touch with this sense of being are "Doing Nothing" and the "Silent Day".   During recovery from compulsive doing, we begin to realize how active we have been in life. We begin to see how, even in attempts to heal ourselves, in the past we have often done more of the same. We may, for instance, have begun to attend seminars and workshops in stress management and taken on extra reading in the area of time management and organization.   We may even have been driven and forced about going to therapy or self-help meetings — crowding them into our busy routine and ending up feeling empty and unfulfilled even *after* the activity was over.

The point is that more *doing* is not what is needed. Unfortunately that is often all society has modeled. If we have a problem, society says the thing to do is "solve" it. We need to get *busy* and find solutions and implement them in life. If we do not, we "aren't really motivated" and we deserve what befalls us! Isn't that the message heard so often?

Healing from compulsive doing allows us to discover, and slowly begin to accept, the paradox that "to do nothing is to do everything". The character Siddhartha in Herman Hesse's famous book by the same name, spent most of his life on a quest for spiritual enlightenment. He tried everything he could think of, from material wealth to physical love to self-denial, all in a search for meaning. Eventually, when he gave up and sat defeated by a river, he discovered himself! He found that all of the things he had been *doing* to find himself only led him further away. Only by *being* (and not trying to *do* anything) did he find what he sought.

Being is a paradox which healing compulsive doers come to understand and to *live from*. Just as alcoholics come to understand that they are unable to "control" drinking and that it has become "unmanageable", so the compulsive doer gradually learns that more work, or even controlling and altering activity patterns is not going to provide healing.

This increased willingness to "just be" also means that the healing compulsive doer is less likely to be acting out to avoid feelings. When healing from compulsive doing, we begin to pay increasing amounts of attention to what we feel inside. Instead of an addiction to work or accomplishing things, we spend more time feeling feelings and sharing them. At first these feelings may seem like weird aliens within, but gradually we learn to listen to them even when we don't know for sure where they will lead. We develop a sense of trust in our destiny and an ability to take up the thread of our feelings knowing that the total fabric will show itself eventually.

As the healing moves along our worklife begins to look very different. We may think back and wonder why we spent so much energy on projects to do and achievements to accomplish when there was so much pleasure and fun available! We no longer feel the *desire* to work so much, or do so much because we have slowly discovered that it means so much and feels so rewarding to just *be*. We begin to realize that compulsive doing was not only a way of playing God by trying to force and control life and destiny, but also a denial of the perfection of creation! We begin to see that we were designed to be just the way that we actually are rather than trying to continually change, or deny who we are.

As we trust our ability to be spontaneous more, we have less tolerance for "shoulds" — the arch enemy of all compulsive doers. We begin to recognize when we are feeling compulsive, and shoulds become our early warning signal. When we start to feel we are "shoulding" on ourselves and externalizing our focus, we take time out to re-tune the listening process. We focus back inside and let go of guilt so that our spontaneous, natural side can re-emerge. The more we give ourselves the right to be who we are the stronger we become.

In compulsive doing there is a sense that we have become "human doings" rather than human beings. We live our days in a sense of what I like to call "linearity". That is, we move from one point to the next like crazed efficiency experts accomplishing what we "should" until the next thing to accomplish presents itself. What's missing is that sense of spontaneity, choicefulness, pacing, and balance. In recovery — like the religious or spiritual pilgrim —

we begin to explore and sense what it means to *be*. We become less linear and dogmatic. We learn to value the process of life rather than always focusing on the goals. We begin to realize that it is the here and now that counts most. That life is a series of moments strung together and that it is here in the present that the real action is happening.

Healthy being is a way of living in the world. It is entirely experiential and different for every individual. The critical aspect of healthy being is spontaneous disinhibition and living from our center. The world is constantly calling us to do, be, or say what we "should." Many feel guilty, or fearful about facing down those external shoulds and saying, "No. This is who I need to be. I have a right to choose. I have a right to be here." When we take up that challenge, we get ourselves onto the road of healthy being.

What can help provide the courage to make the journey from doing to being is the awareness that even a lifetime of material success and good work *pales when compared to even a few hours of true beingness.* When we are brave enough to face down shoulds, we make a contribution to the world that is as real as it is difficult to measure. When you think of the people who have most influenced your life or those you have felt most loved by, it is likely you will find that they had a strong quality of being about them. When we are into beingness, wonderful things begin to happen to us and around us and other people benefit either directly or indirectly.

As part of an ability to live in the moment, we learn the importance of the five senses. In healing we discover that it is those experiences that involve the *senses* that are most enjoyable and that are most real. We become able to be still long enough to appreciate the smell of a spring afternoon, to feel the warm sun in the morning on the way to work, to enjoy the cool water we drink, to make love and take pleasure in the sensuality of the experience, to feel our bodies and sense the messages they have. We begin to see the intrinsic God-given value in what we sense. Our experience becomes a teacher as well as a guide.

Our experience of ourself is connected to an awareness of our body. When we begin to heal from compulsive doing we feel a re-awakening to physical sensuality. Sights, sounds, touches, tastes, temperatures, and smells all become more vibrant. We become aware of the incredible beauty of the world. The simplest pleasures and experiences become cause for celebration. Sleep and food, for example, become intensely pleasurable. *This moment* becomes all that is needed for satisfaction and serenity. Instead of fighting, controlling and caretaking the environment and our bodies, we begin to embrace and accept circumstances and ourselves.

We also discover that *relationships* have been missing, or at least sadly neglected. In the healing process we re-learn what is most important and begin to act on that knowledge. Instead of saying that we value our family most while spending all of our time at the office or working on projects, we actually put time where our values are. As we work through fears of abandonment and rejection we begin to risk reaching out and being vulnerable. We also risk setting boundaries and limits and saying "no" to others when needed. Relationships become healthier and exciting, though not necessarily always smooth. We reach out and let others reach out to us.

As relationships improve we begin to develop more of a sense of self-esteem. Instead of devaluing ourselves we begin to see the natural worth in who we are. We chase away those voices from the past that say that we are not worthy or deserving. We relax more into ourselves and feel more centered and self-possessed. We take pride in our views and opinions and allow others to disagree with them when they need to without trying to prove them wrong.

Eventually we begin to recover a sense of self again and it is a wonderful experience. For the first time we begin to feel "solid". We begin to really feel at home with ourselves. Because our identity and sense of purpose are no longer outside of us (embodied in what is done and accomplished) we feel paradoxically more self-ownership. It becomes easier to manage time, and listen to our bodies when they are indicating we are hungry, tired, or unfulfilled. Choices become easier to make because we ask ourselves how we *feel* internally and wait for the answer to arise. We take time for ourself because it feels good to do so, not because we were told we "should" by some stress management book. In essence, we come home to ourselves by giving up what we *believed* would eventually save us — our compulsion to do.

Coming home to ourselves is a wonderful feeling. In the midst of compulsive doing we may even have stopped believing that we still exist. It sounds funny, but many recovering compulsive doers will say that they had even forgotten what it *felt* like to be themselves! Recovering from compulsive doing means finding our identity as people again. We recover the person we were meant to be.

As someone who has been traveling this road I can assure you that you *are* still the wonderful human being that you started out to be. When you begin to recover your sense of really *being*, you will know this is true. You probably have already had moments, hours, or days when you have been able to let go of compulsive doing and felt really at peace. At those times you may have experienced a sense of serenity and wholeness, a sense of somehow being different. Instead of feeling separate from the world and other people, through attempts to control them, such moments bring a sense of flowing — of being part of life in a deeply spiritual and fulfilling way. When we are deep into compulsive doing, it helps to remember that sense of serenity is always there *inside* waiting for us to shift perspectives and behaviors enough so that it can *come out*.

We have looked thus far at what it's like to recover our sense of being and the inner aliveness that comes as a result of this qualitative shift. Another healthy change that occurs as a result of recovery from compulsive doing is release from controlling and caretaking.

As the family of origin was explored (see Chapter Five) we may have found that we learned to be a compulsive doer, should-er, or accomplisher in order to cope with or solve our family's internal problems. For example, as a child we may have been able to sense that our parents were uncomfortable with us — cold and distant and seemingly disinterested. We may have also noticed that they seemed to value getting things done around the house. In fact, every time someone brought up feelings around the home, dad and mom would get very busy! So we decided that doing things was an acceptable way of getting approval, relating to others and handling emotions. As a result, we became compulsive controllers of the environment.

As compulsive doing progressed, we may have noticed there was a similarity between control of the environment and control of people. We found ourself caretaking, controlling, and "shoulding on" everyone else in much the same way we did these things to ourself. The more we did so, the more we felt out of control or, more accurately, under the control of others. In healing we discover that to control someone else, to caretake or fix them, *is to be controlled by them.* Again, we learn an important paradox: when we control others we lose our identity in them. As we let go of control we find, to our delight, that life can largely take care of itself. We develop the awareness of being participants in a river of relationships that we can either fight against or let go into and flow with. We begin to choose flowing more often than fighting.

A word or two is in order here about the importance of close, intimate, adult relationships in the process of moving towards healthy being. Marriage and other intimate relationships can be thought of as contexts for growth. Many people believe that marriage is supposed to be a finished product as soon as the marital vows are spoken. Nothing could be further from the truth. Often the *real* work of a marriage does not begin until years later when conflicts begin to arise in the middle years of the relationship. That is the time when it becomes apparent that primary intimate relationships *by design* are there to push buttons and help us grow.

The most intimate relationships serve to draw out and accentuate the inner conflicts from our family of origin including compulsive doing. If, out of fear, we blame the onset of these issues on our partner we just become further stuck in them. If, on the other hand, we courageously embrace and take ownership of them we can catapult ourselves into further growth.

As we become more secure in our individual power of being it becomes easier to let go of blaming our partner and take ownership of issues. We stop fighting and begin to fearlessly flow with the process of the relationship. Our significant other then acts as a catalyst for developing our beingness.

Recovering compulsive doers know that it's okay to detach from others, much in the same way we detach from controlling the environment. We begin to trust our own counsel about things and to feel okay about not always being right. We also do not need to have others conform to our beliefs and values. It's still nice when they do, but we realize that personal identity is not tied up in that of another. We begin to rediscover the capacity to love through an expanded ability to accept others for who they are — but not before we love ourselves for who *we* are. As we are more true to ourselves and let go of what others think of us, we are more free to reach out *as ourselves* to others.

As the power of being grows inside we begin to have an increasingly healing impact on those within the family circle. Family meals, for example, can be leisurely, playful, and supportive. Parents who are compulsive doers tend to encourage "grab and go" meals. Power of being parents are comfortable enough with feelings and individuality to want to actually sit down with their children and share a lengthy meal.

Such experiences will help these children to develop a sense that they are wanted, loved, and valued. When they go out into the world they will walk more peacefully carrying a sense of their own power of being. While some people fear that developing choicefulness and self ownership results in narcism and self-indulgence, the opposite is true. Our healing affects those closest and they in turn affect others. By loving ourself we create love in our families and their families.

Another healthy pattern that begins to emerge as we heal from compulsive doing lies in the ability to make choices and decisions. Making choices can be excruciatingly painful when we are trying to make them perfectly, or on the basis of external information only. When we begin to recover our selves, we instinctively are able to make decisions and choose options which are healthy and are in tune with our inner rhythms. We become able to slow down enough to listen to our inner voice — that protective inner guidance system we all have.

At any time during the day we are able to ask this inner voice what is the right choice and then wait for an answer. We do this instead of forcing, shoulding, or pushing into things that are not right, but look good from a compulsive doing perspective. Eventually we become more spontaneous and able to rethink plans based on how we feel at that moment.

We also increasingly realize that choices are not as important as choosing to accept what *is* in each moment. Instead of being caught up in decisions about where to eat and what to work on next, we focus on letting go into what we are *currently* experiencing. We realize that our desire to control and force life blocks the ability to simply experience the beauty of this moment and whatever it brings.

This in turn tends to make us less materialistic. We spend less time looking for things to make us happy. We realize that nurturance is here right now in everything that we are doing. Life is set up so we don't have to go looking for new adventures and experiences — they are with us now. Certainly we will have adventures and make forward progress in our life. We will also enjoy the process of that forward motion by living as completely as possible in each moment as it passes.

The healing process also leads us to look more closely at *how* we do things rather than *what* we do. As acting out compulsive doers we are excellent at manipulating the environment. Unfortunately, managing the *content* of life causes us to regress back into compulsive doing most times. Instead, we need to look at *how* we are living. In compulsive doing recovery we focus on the quality of the experience rather than the quantity of what we accomplish.

For example, many people like to exercise in the morning before going to work. For compulsive doers working out can either be "work", or it can be nurturing play — depending on *how* it's done. If we decide upon an arbitrary amount and type of exercise and then *force* ourselves through the motions of doing the "routine" it becomes lifeless and compulsive. We emerge from what could have been an energizing and healthy experience feeling harried and stressed.

In compulsive doing recovery the exercise *process* becomes the goal. We choose exercise based on how we are feeling that morning and are willing to modify the workout to fit with how we are feeling as we go along. We do what feels best. If we would rather go out for a run because it's a nice sunny morning, that's what we do. If we feel like we need to spend time getting connected to our body through slow floor exercises and breathing practice we do that. We become flexible and spontaneous. The activity (whatever it is) is used to get more in touch with our inner rhythm and pacing.

Another critical shift that happens is the release of shame about who we are as people. As we become more in touch with the power of being we begin to chip away at the wall of shame that has built up around compulsive doing. We spend less time feeling like there is something wrong with us, or that we do not have a right to be here. We spend more time being ourself, whoever that may be.

Because many compulsive doers tend to function in a "hero" role, shame is an intense issue in recovery. In recovery we realize that we do not need to be perfect and we find a sense of acceptance for our natural traits as an individual. We find a sense of *forgiveness* for ourself and can continue to accept needs, likes, dislikes, successes and mistakes as we move through life. Being perfect loses its interest and acceptance takes its place in our value system.

In healing we discover that just as we are happily imperfect, so is everyone around us. We experience the liberation that comes from being just a normal person like everyone else. Our sense of shame drops away and we realize increasingly that we are okay just as we are. We learn that we are not more valuable, or less valuable than others. We find that we have a right to exist and to just be alive.

As recovering compulsive doers we are able to accept and learn from modeling and mentoring. If you have children, you have probably observed that they seldom do what you *tell* them, but they do follow your *example*. For better or for worse, modeling is how humans learn. Just as we became compulsive doers in part from watching our parents and significant others, we recover the ability to *be* by watching non-compulsive doers, or recovering compulsive doers. In our healing we are increasingly able to select role models that are nurturing and positive. We then internalize the healthy behaviors which we observe them participating in.

Healing from compulsive doing is a process. The healing does not happen overnight and we, as imperfect humans, will not always be able to maintain a healthy balance. It's important to remember that, while we *can* learn to abstain from compulsive doing, we cannot abstain from work and activity. This makes recovery a balancing act that is often tricky to master. We are likely to find ourselves frequently in ambivalent situations. The quality of healing is measured in part by how well we have learned to balance doing behavior. We cannot live in a healthy manner in society without this sense of balance.

What assists here is a courageous willingness to view compulsive doing as a real *addiction*. As we practice living in balance we begin to sense power to say "No" when we feel the pull of compulsive doing. Shoulds become a warning sign that we are out of balance and we take these warnings seriously. We learn that the discovery of who we want to be and what we need lies on the other side of that "No" to shoulds. We gradually design a lifestyle that supports that balanced awareness.

Sometimes, too, we will find ourselves in real crisis. We will have times where we deplete our resources so greatly, or run into a new fear so overwhelming, that we panic and lose our sense of self. It feels rotten at the time and we may be tempted to kick ourselves, but it is important to take heart. There is no compulsive doer who is not cycling in and out of difficulty. We spiral between being controlled by shoulds and feeling free to choose who we want to be and what we want to do. That process may look something like this:

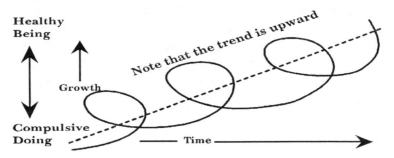

The difference, as we get closer to the power of being, is that the crises get a little less nasty and a little farther apart each time. We spend more and more time in healthy serenity and balance and feel spontaneous energy more frequently.

One last issue deserves mention here. A powerful way of viewing the healing process is through the concept of *polarities*. Polarities are found everywhere in life. Opposites of strength and weakness, anger and affection, day and night, and right and wrong, are all present in life and relationships.

Some of the polarities which recovering compulsive doers develop a sensitivity to and an appreciation for are listed   below. If you are a recovering compulsive doer and are moving from the *left* side of the polarities below toward the *right,* you are headed in the correct direction. If you are headed in the *other* direction it is a good time to go back into the lifestyle changes described in Chapter Six.

POLARITIES IN COMPULSIVE DOING

DOING . . . . BEING
EXTERNALIZING INTERNALIZING
REFUSING . . . . EMBRACING
SHOULDS . . . . WANT TOS
ANALYZING . . . . . EXPERIENCING
YOU CHOOSE . . . . I CHOOSE
DEPENDENT . . SELF-POSSESSED
HOLDING ON . . . . . . DETACHING
COMPLEX . . . . SIMPLE
UNCENTERED . . . . . . CENTERED
CARETAKING . . . . SELF-OWNING
CONTROL . . . . SPONTANEITY
INHIBITION . . . . . DISINHIBITION
PERSISTANCE . . . . . ACCEPTANCE
TENSION . . . . RELAXATION
FORCING . . . . SURRENDER
BLAMING . . . . OWNING
CONTROLLING . . . . LETTING GO
FEAR . . . . COURAGE

In reviewing the above polarities notice that many of the recovery suggestions put forward in Chapter Six lead directly to the characteristics on the *right.* Compulsive doing robs these qualities of healthy functioning.

In conclusion, keep in mind that healing from compulsive doing is a process and it is the *process itself* which we come to cherish. The goal of healing is not to "accomplish" something, but rather to experience qualitative differences in how we are living *right now*. As we get further into the healing process we may even develop a sense of thankfulness for compulsive doing because of the powerful insights it propels us toward.

A Zen poem expresses well this process of rebirth through destruction: "My barn having burned to the ground, I can now see the moon."

Without the struggle of compulsive doing, we are less likely to appreciate the sweetness and aliveness of healthy being.

EPILOGUE:
"REJOINING THE FLEET"

YOUR POWER OF BEING
IN THE WORLD

W ith Chapter Seven the original purpose of this book — to point the reader in the direction of a very special voyage from doing to being — is completed. As the power of being becomes more a part of life, however, it is natural to begin to seek ways to bring this experience back into the world and share it with others in some way. The journey is not fully complete until we return to the community and find some way of expressing our being in the world.

This can be a *very* challenging step for compulsive doers. It is all too easy to get tempted back into *doing* for doing's sake and lose the sense of beingness. Even those who have been working a lifetime towards the power of being share this difficulty. Even when one has arrived in a state of being it is easy to get lost back in doing because the essential call of the world is toward *action*. It is difficult to bring back from the voyage that quality of being to share with others. For many of us travelers it is even more challenging a task than recovering the power to be. Sharing the power of being is very important, however, since it is something which is in short supply in our culture today. We need more being to balance the overload of doing we have created.

One of the aspects that makes the diagnosis of compulsive doing so elusive and the behavior so difficult to deal with is that our culture has become acclimated to it. We are a society which values production, achievement and "getting the job done". It has become normal to over work and focus on doing to the exclusion of being. We have, in a sense, become addicted to work and forgotten how to play for the sake of play.

One of the interesting things you may have noticed about the Over Doing It Screening Test presented in Chapter Two is that it would be almost impossible to obtain a score of zero. Yet, all of the items on the ODIST are clearly indicators of compulsive doing. What this suggests is we have, as a culture, accomodated levels of compulsive doing that, while *comparatively* "normal" are not *healthy*. This epilogue is intended to point out the effect that individual struggles with compulsive doing can have on society as a whole as we return to the world with a power of being.

Obsessive-compulsive folks begin healing by focusing internally. In the recovery process we look deeply at our own experience and feelings and regain a sense of the ability to *be* — spontaneously and naturally. Once we have done so, we are able to carry that sense of self-ownership out into the world. We gradually become able to share that developed quality of beingness with others. As we do so they in turn have an opportunity to become aware of their own potential to harness the power of being. The more that follow this course the more we will re-balance *society's* tendencies to over do and over work. This is essential. Society must regain the ability to *be* or we will continue to see an escalation in stress-related physical and environmental problems and a decrease in the ability to love and *accept* one another.

This suggestion is in direct disagreement with those authors (Machlowitz, 1980) who assert that compulsive doing can be *functional* and that compulsive doers are "remarkably satisfied". While it is obvious that *work* itself is a necessary and important part of life, compulsive doing *is* non-functional and leads to early spiritual and even physical death. (I believe it says something important, and not very positive, about our culture that there are authors who would even suggest that it is otherwise.)

It's interesting that few people (except active alcoholics refusing to acknowledge their illness) would suggest that alcoholism is, or can be, functional and healthy. We do, however, hear this assertion frequently regarding compulsive working. As is the case with alcohol, I believe we must separate between the substance, or process itself (e.g., work, doing activities) which is not in itself harmful at all and obsessive-compulsive doing which *is*.

How can society justify the assertion that compulsive doing is functional and healthy? From an objective, sociological viewpoint there might be some merit to this idea. In the same sense we might say that alcohol addiction is "functional" in that it helps people to experience less subjective distress when confronted with stressful life situations. Compulsive doing too helps to avoid uncomfortable feelings and awareness. If we take this approach, however, where will we end up? If we do not turn to face fears and feelings, they eventually hunt us down.

If we are given to denial about something, we merge it, adopting an altered perspective on reality. For example, until recently society was in denial about the extent and seriousness of the sexual abuse in families. Today few informed people would say that incest and other forms of child sexual abuse are not extremely damaging and all too common. Only a few years ago, however, the problem was by-and-large passed over. That is, until those that suffered from child sexual abuse began to bravely come forward and bring the problem out into the open.

I believe that society is acclimated to compulsive doing and has even come to praise it. Only the subjective experiential suffering of the compulsive doer reminds us of the damaging nature of this addiction. Just as society awakened gradually to the destructive effects of alcoholism and other forms of substance abuse on the individual, family, and society, we must now open our eyes to the unhealthy realities of *process* compulsions such as workaholism, Type-A behavior, and compulsive doing.

Let us take the analysis of the destructive effects of compulsive doing beyond the individual and out into society. The goal is to look at ways in which compulsive doing and addiction to work affects the quality of life in society, and consequently, on the planet.

There are a wide variety of statistics now available which attest to the negative impact and personal, financial, and environmental costs of alcohol addiction in a wide variety of areas. Most of the information we now have regarding compulsive doing's destructive impact comes from the field of stress and "burnout" (Millon, Green and Meagher, 1982; Goldberger and Breznitz, 1982). Researchers in this area have linked stress to a wide range of physical and social problems including: disrupted sleep, elevated cholesterol levels, high and low blood pressure, job dissatisfaction and employee turnover, fatigue, depression, sexual maladjustment, interpersonal alienation, job burnout, arthritis, early retirement, rate of smoking and caffeine intake, inferior work product, on-the-job accidents, employee theft, heart disease, cerebral accidents, arthritis, headache and backache, respiratory illness, dermatitis, diabotes, lowered immune response, increased mortality rate, peptic ulcer, and suicide (Goldberger and Breznitz, 1982). Whew!

It isn't difficult to see that, apart from the personal suffering involved, there is a significant cost to society as well. From huge financial drains on businesses and corporations as a result of accidents, lawsuits, employee turnover, sick leave, etc., to the social damage resulting from deterioration in families, the price of stress and its by-products is staggering.

Research studies are even now showing that over working and Type-A behavior (see Chapter Three) are causing long-term problems in the nation's corporations. Pace (1988) reports in his study that Type-A managers are more likely to be stress-prone, addicted to other substances, and a detriment to employee involvement in the corporation. Their tendency toward impatience, irritation, and aggression is seen as having a negative impact on the corporation as a whole.

Homer (1985) indicates in his study of worker burnout that the burnout phenomena seen increasingly in American corporations is a result of a stressful work environment combined with an *individual's* obsessive-compulsive response to a particular environment. Spruell (1987) reports that even though there may be "short-lived" benefits of compulsive work behavior (e.g., increased production) these "benefits" come at the sacrifice of long-term organizational gains. Nagy (1985) also concludes that high workaholism levels and Type-A behavior are directly related to employee burnout. It is apparent from these studies and others that compulsive doing and/or Type-A behavior are linked to long-term problems in the workplace.

Let us turn now to a wider view of the impact of compulsive doing and stress on the total *environment* in which we reside. We have discussed some of the ways that personal compulsive doing tendencies expand outward into the corporations and organizations which we work within. These systems and organization in turn have an important impact on the planet and its environmental systems.

As we look at this process it may be helpful to visualize compulsive doing as a tumor in the body of humanity. The tumor begins at a specific site, but can spread throughout the various organs and systems of the body, eventually resulting in the body's destruction.

Lester R. Brown and his colleagues at the Worldwatch Institute (1990) produce a yearly scientific report on the condition of the body of humanity called the *State of the World*. In this report, Institute researchers look at a variety of indicators of progress or deterioration in the planet's environmental status. In a recent issue of the report Brown concludes that "The fundamental changes we have outlined in forestry, agriculture and other physical systems cannot occur *without corresponding shifts in the social, economic, and moral character of human societies.* During the transition to sustainability, political leaders and citizens alike will be forced to *reevaluate* their goals and aspirations, to redefine their measures of success, and to *adjust work and leisure to a new set of principles* that have at their core the welfare of future generations." (Brown, et al, 1990: pp. 187-188.)

What will this "shift" to a "new set of principles" look like? It will look very much like what we have been calling healthy being. Let's allow this to sink in for a moment.   What is suggested is that the behaviors we need to create a healthy and sustainable future on this planet are the *very behaviors which arise naturally from the power of being* (as outlined in Chapters Six and Seven of this book).   The destructive impact of the national obsession with doing, accomplishing, and forced "productiveness" goes beyond the individual to impact upon society and then in turn upon the physical planet itself. Living out of the power of being has a natural healing effect as we reach out to the world with acceptance.

To illustrate, let us view some of the more readily apparent ways that compulsive doing can affect the world around us.   One of the characteristics of compulsive doers, especially those with high ODIST scores, is the tendency to *create* more work! Just as an alcoholic contributes to the production of alcohol by stimulating, through his or her purchases, companies to produce more alcohol, so the compulsive doer stimulates production of more work. This work is often not necessary or functional and is likely to be redundant, and marked by repetitious errors. Since the goal is to *work*, not to *complete work*, the compulsive doer becomes caught up in, and creates, seemingly endless cycles of productivity — the actual "product" of which is more work.

What is this cyclical nature of compulsive doing likely to do to society and environment?   What happens is that compulsive doers stimulate more activity on the part of others. Co-workers and office staff become harried extensions of the compulsive doer's ambition. Peers become stimulated to keep up with the accomplishments of the compulsive doer. Inevitably the entire sphere of influence of the compulsive doer becomes altered toward greater, often non-functional, productivity. This productivity, in turn, requires the consumption of all types of material resources from the environment, depending on the work being generated. Eventually these resources become depleted, just as the psychophysiological coping resources of the compulsive doer's body become depleted and, over time, result in stress, burnout, and exhaustion.

If you are a compulsive doer it may help at this point to take a look at your own life in the light of the above picture. In particular, mentally compare the periods of time when you have been most compulsive about what you did and the times when you have been feeling more peaceful, serene and in touch with your power of being. Make a list of the material and social resources you "burned up" during your compulsive doing periods as opposed to your more healthy periods.

Do you see a difference? During the periods of recovery did you tend to drive less? Were you more likely to use public transportation, make fewer costly mistakes, buy fewer unnecessary things, use less paper, take more time to recycle and re-use materials, run less water, use less electricity, burn less fuel, be less materialistic, eat less food (especially fast-food), jam fewer telephone lines, and use less health care?

The above behaviors are consistent with the fundamental changes recommended by organizations monitoring the global environment (Hollander, 1990; Brown, et al, 1990). Compulsive doing behaviors are not! If we look beyond the individual to society in a more general sense we see that the acclimation to compulsive doing has caused a gigantic increase in material resource consumption. Why, for example, does the United States (a nation renowned for its dedication to the work ethic) consume the lion's share of the planet's resources? Do we really *need* all of those resources, or are we *addicted* to them via the compulsive patterns of doing?

We have difficulty as a society answering these kinds of questions because of a collective denial about our culture's obsessive-compulsive character. It's a cliche that people visiting from other, less compulsive societies often talk about "those pushy, demanding Americans" almost in the same way that fellow patrons at a bar will talk about the alcoholic's singleminded dedication to the bottle. Perhaps, coming from a context outside our own, they are able to see something we cannot. Perhaps they can see our consumptive tendencies more clearly. Perhaps some of them see our compulsive doing for what it is.

As individuals act out compulsive doing the larger organizations and systems of which they are a part are impacted. Many corporate entities have become acclimated to compulsive doing and are paying the price both internally and externally. Internal costs come in the form of increased errors, high employee turnover, escalating health insurance costs, and expensive "down time". External costs to the environment are magnified by the size of the corporation and the extent of material resources demanded. Where the individual compulsive doer can impact air quality to some degree by excessive trips in the car, the addictive organization can *dramatically* damage the environment through the output of toxic waste into the air, water and land.

Ann Wilson Schaef and Diane Fassel in *The Addictive Organization* (1988) illustrate well the destructive force of the work addictive company. Oil spills, toxic waste production, polluted air, and depleted land and human resources are easily overlooked as the organization rushes toward greater productivity, achievement, and material acquisition. Members of the organization who stop to ask "Where is all this heading?" meet with disapproval and incredulity on the part of their colleagues.

It is becoming apparent that society can no longer sustain the level of compulsive doing to which we have become acclimated. As a society we have become increasingly concerned about the state of environment. We have also developed an awareness of the degree of stress overload that we are experiencing as individuals and the need for an answer to the "stress crisis" that we find ourselves in. What we don't realize is it isn't enough to initiate home recycling and attend stress management workshops. As individuals and as a society, we need to begin to address the addictive process that *underlies* this behavior. Without going on the difficult journey back to being our efforts may, in fact, just throw more gasoline on the fire.

The process of social and organizational addiction to doing is much the same as that seen in the individual. When we know the *purpose* of the addiction (the avoidance of painful feelings and experiences), the mechanics of the process become clear. Diane Fassel (1990) points out that we are living in a society that is painful. Starvation, poverty, sickness, violent crime, homelessness, the threat of nuclear holocaust, and the destruction of the environment are *painful*. Do we *feel* this pain as we rush off to work in the morning? Or do we find ourselves saying, "I don't have *time* to worry about those things! I need to get this project completed by Friday!" Compulsive doing allows us to soothe and avoid both personal pain *and* the pain and suffering that surrounds us on this planet.

The trouble is, when we *avoid* something we never get to a solution. Do we really believe that increased *productivity* is going to solve the problems of our society? Sure, technology and innovation are important. Certainly it is desirable to have a healthy personal and national economy. But is that what is really happening, or are we getting further and further into debt on all levels of society? Is compulsive doing causing us to "write checks that we cannot pay for" (both literally and figuratively)? It is important to deal with this addiction in order to survive as a society.

Healing from compulsive doing is a personal matter. It begins with the individual. As we practice the principles put forward in this book we begin to heal ourselves. As we heal internally our outward expressions begin to change. Others begin to observe and model our healthy self-care behaviors and may themselves seek out the power of being. We have more time to care for the environment. We begin to let go of a consumer orientation. We think more in terms of satisfaction and serenity than accomplishing and acquiring. We encourage the organizations we belong to to share resources and knowledge, and to think more in terms of environmental and social protection. In short, we become an agent of healing as a natural expression of *our own* journey to being.

As part of the discussion that takes place during workshops and talks on THE POWER OF BEING, participants often share fears that they will be able to have little or no real impact on the world around them. It is not uncommon to hear "Even if I discover my power of being it won't change anything. The world is too far gone in the direction of compulsive doing."

These are certainly valid and justified concerns. The balance of society is tipped very much in favor of compulsive approaches to living. Looking at the situation from the point of view that the environment *has* to change for us to feel better easily brings on feelings of fear and resignation. Fortunately, the power of being approach is very different from this! When we are living out of the power of being our whole perspective on life changes. No longer do we view the world as imperfect. The process of living itself becomes a joy and our inner delight *naturally expands outward* through our actions and relationships.

Thus, we impact our world through the altering of our perspective. We do not go out with the intention to change everything. Rather, through our own personal growth, we come to regard ourselves with such acceptance and peace that our quality of living affects the world! The journey begins within. It is enough to live out of our beingness. When we do that we will NATURALLY extend spontaneity and love out into the world.

In our healing we become empowered to heal the environment. As others join this process the healing expands and extends outward. Eventually (not soon, but eventually) the destructive force of compulsive doing can be redirected toward the protection and recovery of the planet. The powerful addiction to doing, accomplishing, and shoulding can become an investment in the power of being. We will find ways to bring back to the world what we have found inside our own lives.

Of course, none of this is going to occur, or even make much sense until we have actually experienced *the power of being*. It is difficult to imagine the effect simply changing the way in which we approach the world can have until we have walked down that road a while. For now we need to trust that we *are* on the right road and that good things will grow from the healthy seeds we are planting. We need to trust in our voyage to the power of being.

AFTERWORD

Throughout this book it has been suggested that compulsive doing is an unhealthy *process* which we get into out of fear of being *ourselves*. Self ownership, disinhibition, and letting go into natural impulses and rhythms are the opposite of compulsive doing. These qualities of living can be wonderful. Life with the power of being can be ecstatic and filled with pleasure. The journey from compulsive doing to disinhibited spontaneity is a difficult one, but one well worth taking. Besides, what else have you got to do?

To all those on this voyage, I wish you well and I hope that in some small way this book may serve as encouragement and support for your travels. If, like mine, your ship of compulsive doing runs aground from time to time, it is my hope that you will find a new wind of healing in your life. That wind can take you to wonderful places, feelings, and relationships. It can bring you in touch with your own *power of being*!

APPENDIX A

SOME QUESTIONS FOR CHRISTIAN KOMOR

In his breakthrough book *THE POWER OF BEING FOR PEOPLE WHO DO TOO MUCH*, psychologist Christian R. Komor, Psy.D. shares a simple and powerful message: Our society has become acclimated to unhealthy levels of compulsive working, accomplishing and shoulding. In his book, Dr. Komor provides surprising insights into how this trend toward workaholism began, how we can tell the extent to which we personally have been affected, the possible physical, emotional, social and environmental consequences of compulsive approaches to living, and what we can do to heal ourselves. In so doing, he introduces us to what he calls *THE POWER OF BEING* and specific techniques for achieving it.

WHAT EXACTLY IS "COMPULSIVE DOING?"

In many ways it is similar to what other people are calling workaholism, "hurry sickness", Type-A Behavior, or perfectionism. Compulsive doing is the tendency to do what we think we should do instead of what we choose to do. Compulsive doing is a lifestyle in which the demands of the environment gradually take precedence over internal feelings, needs, and responses. In the end, compulsive shoulds take over and we lose the ability to be spontaneous and uninhibited. In a sense life gets turned inside out so that what is external becomes more important that what is internal.

COMPULSIVE DOING AS YOU DESCRIBE IT SOUNDS LIKE A VIRTUE. WHY IS IT SUCH A PROBLEM?

If we look around at the way the world is currently, we see that what is happening is that both on the level of the individual and as a society we are hitting the ceiling in terms of the amount of stress that we can handle. Most of the major illnesses of our generation are stress related to one degree or another. Also, the environment is undeniably showing signs of excessive wear and tear. Excessive stress is the result of pushing too hard, over-running physical and environmental coping resources and then reaching a point of exhaustion. That is what is happening today and it ought to scare the dickens out of us! Once physical and environmental health is eroded, it's pretty tough to get back.

I really see it as the difference between being self-centered, and being centered in your self. If I am living out of my spontaneous being self I will naturally take action that enhances life and the lives of others. That's part of the power of being and the reason it is so important now. If we are all more grounded in this aspect of living many of the problems we have would simply fade away.

HOW DOES A PERSON KNOW IF THEY ARE REALLY DOING TOO MUCH, OR JUST BEING OVERWORKED BY THEIR JOB, ETC.?

One of the most obvious ways is by looking to see if the activity and lifestyle we are involved in is coming out of a sense of choicefulness, or a sense of goal-oriented drivenness. Many people have the idea that life is filled with things that we need to get done. The truth is that at its essence, life is entirely optional. Ultimately, if you think about it, we don't even have to stay alive if we don't want to. Yet so many live as if everything we get into is a should.

To recover the power of being, we first need to acknowledge the possibility of choicefulness in life. The difficult truth is that even the most valuable task or endeavor loses it's inherent worth when done without a true sense of desire and spontaneity. Even things that are supposed to be "recreational", or just for "fun" can become part of the problem. There are many stressed-out "playaholics" out there with piles of toys and no sense of being.

IS THERE A TEST YOU CAN TAKE TO FIND OUT IF YOU ARE A COMPULSIVE DOER?

Well, as a matter of fact, there are several currently available. The one that I offer in the book is called the **Over Doing It Screening Test**. It contains a variety of questions which give a practical sense for where an individual is on the continuum from healthy being to compulsive doing. For me a good "test" is to look at whether my voice, laugh, and smile seem to be natural and spontaneous, or forced and dead. Another good indicator of compulsive doing is loss of enjoyment of life's basics such as sleeping, having sex, eating, and just being part of nature. If we aren't able to cry from the ecstacy of just watching the sun shining on the clouds, or a tree blowing in the breeze there is more being potential to which we have not yet awakened ourselves.

IN YOUR BOOK YOU TALK ABOUT LIST MAKING AS ONE POTENTIAL PROBLEM AREA?

Yes. The list making that many of us do is a good example of the difference between healthy choicefulness and compulsive doing. The critical questions is "Do I own my list, or does *it* own me?" Lots of people make lists of things to do. The problem comes when that list becomes only a means to an end rather than an expression of an internal process of selecting options for what we would like to do and what feels most important. In so doing we externalize that list and give it a power over us that it shouldn't have.

YOU HAVE SUGGESTED THAT THE REMEDY FOR COMPULSIVE DOING IS SOMETHING CALLED HEALTHY BEING. COULD YOU DESCRIBE MORE WHAT YOU MEAN BY HEALTHY BEING?

Healthy being is a way of living in the world. It is entirely experiential and different for every individual. The critical aspect of healthy being is what I think of as "spontaneous disinhibition." The world is constantly calling us to do, be, or say what we "should." Many feel guilty, or fearful about facing down those external shoulds and saying, "No. This is who I need to be. I have a right to choose. I have a right to be here." When we take up that challenge, we get ourselves onto the road of healthy being.

What can help to make this jump from doing to being is the awareness that even a lifetime of material success and good works pales when compared to even a few hours of true beingness. When we are brave enough to face down shoulds we make a contribution to the world that is as real as it is difficult to measure. When you think of the people who have most influenced your life or those you have felt most loved by, it is likely they had a strong quality of being about them. When we are into our beingness, wonderful things begin to happen to us and around us and other people benefit either directly or indirectly.

HOW DOES ONE GET FROM COMPULSIVE DOING TO HEALTHY BEING?

First of all it isn't something that you "get" to. Being is a quality which is already inside right this moment. We are born with it. The real task, the journey that my book talks about, is getting beneath the layers of compulsivity and denial of self which we build around us. When we do, the power of being naturally emerges. Many self-help books are out there encouraging you to add something more to yourself. My idea is that what you really need to be at peace with this life is inside you all the time. It's a question of discovery and uncovery so to speak.

Now there are some specific areas we can address and techniques which we can use to find the way back to the power of being. In the book I talk about a number of them, including such things as: using fear as a compass, centering, silent days, wandering, activity zones, relaxation boundaries, pacing, surrender, doing nothing, less as more, feelings, disinhibition, and of course, shoulds. So far I have come up with about 70 different techniques and I'm sure there are plenty more.

HOW DID YOU BECOME INVOLVED IN THIS TYPE OF WORK?

Well, to me this is very sacred work and not something one signs up for voluntarily! Back in 1984 I was having a terrible time with the issue of workaholism in my life. At the time I didn't know the difference between compulsive doing and healthy being, or choicefulness. I still struggle in this area more than I would like. So this is a very personal thing for me.

As I have grown and worked with these issues, I have also become convinced that there is incredible potential here for many people and the world in general. As I have mentioned, if more people were approaching the world out of a sense of beingness, many of the stress related illnesses and environmental difficulties would naturally resolve. I'd like to be able to share with everyone some part of this power of being.

APPENDIX B

SOME STRESS MANAGEMENT TOOLS FOR COMPULSIVE DOERS

1. Set manageable goals that fit your needs.

2. Put things in their places. Organization can be relaxing.

3. Get your finances in order. Develop a calm and well-balanced spending plan.

4. Find a "secret retreat" away from your usual daily routine. Get away from it all.

5. Take time to get in touch with feelings before responding to problems or requests.

6.   Affirm yourself. Write your own affirmations, or purchase one of the books of affirmations available.

7.   Realize that "conflict is opportunity". See challenges in that light.

8.   Live in the present. Set goals for the future. Understand the past.

9.   Prepare for the next day so that you will have more time for yourself in the morning.

10. Focus on what you *want* rather than resisting what you do not want.

11. Always gather the facts before making a decision.

12. Always try to simplify when possible. Complications lead to stress.

13. Learn to recognize stressful thoughts. Choose to redirect attention to relaxing thoughts.

14. Let go of black-and-white thinking which leads to stress.

15. Plan ahead. Make sure you have what you need when you need it, to avoid stressful mistakes.

16. Use the healing power of laughter. View life through humorous eyes whenever possible.

17. Realize that you "get what you pay for". If you spend all your time working and accomplishing what you get is a great deal accomplished. If you practice playing you'll get better at it.

18. Try not to escalate problems with "always" and "never" statements. Don't catastrophize.

19. Make sure that each day you do something just for you. Give yourself time for pleasure.

20. Do difficult tasks when you are likely to be freshest.

21. Want what you have now. Trying to achieve the "good life" may be bad for your health. Do you want to have "accomplished" things, or to be happy?

22. Try to use moderation whenever possible. It leads to greater balance. When in crisis do not make sudden moves.

23. "Compartmentalize" whenever possible. Keep work in one area of the house, or at a particular time.

24. Develop a sense of acceptance for all things.

25. Share housework with others you live with. Make up a workable list of chores and stick to it.

26. Don't waste your energy trying to be "perfect". Be who you are.

27. Plan "dates" with your friends, spouse, etc. Write them in your schedule and keep them.

28. Schedule your time appropriately. Don't try to fit too much in, or double book yourself.

29. See the "big picture". Often the fine print just adds confusion.

30. Stop trying to be "first". Try going for the bronze.

31. Focus on the positive. "Don't" never did anything.

32. Remember that sometimes things just heal themselves.

33. If something in your physical environment doesn't work, fix it or get it replaced rather than let it annoy you.

34. Accept the things you cannot change, have courage to change the things you can, and ask God for the wisdom to know the difference!

35. Dare to "screw up!"

36. Stay in touch with your breathing. Use it as a cue to your stress level and a path toward relaxation.

37. Get to know how you "perform" under pressure. Use this awareness to head off potential problems.

38. Let your boss and co-workers know that you are human. Try not to appear invincible. Let them know you have another life that is important to you.

39. When in doubt, trust your senses. You know what is right for you.

40. Try not to own other people's problems. Realize they are responsible for their own lives and issues.

41. Get a telephone answering machine and use it.

42. See yourself, and other "grown-ups" as big kids playing in a very large sandbox. Play.

43. Don't waste energy trying to be someone else. You are you and have a right to value yourself as you are.

44. Realize it is okay to ask for assistance. Use the help of professionals when necessary.

APPENDIX C

HELPFUL REMINDERS FROM WORKAHOLICS ANONYMOUS

I refuse to rush.

The slower I go, the more I do, the more time I have.

Stretch out the work — do less in more time.

Think timelessness — sip not gulp.

Clicks not clocks.

Is this the plan?

Slow is beautiful and powerful / I move glacially.

Am I a human being or a human doing?   Am I enjoying or enduring?

I don't have time not to have time.

When I take time I make time.

By not doing, all is accomplished.

I'm not livin' if I'm driven.

Hail to the snail - simmer, savor, saunter, stroll.

My body keeps score.

My life is full and underscheduled.

Rest is the best reward I can give myself.

Let go — stop trying to run the show.

Success is the quality of your journey.

Enjoyment is my way of keeping score.

The goal is the excuse for the fun of the race.

Take an emergency leisurely.

The more you take your time, the more time you have to take.

Work is the highest form of play.

I do everything easily and effortlessly.

For more information on workaholism recovery, contact: Workaholics Anonymous, PO Box 661501, Los Angeles, CA 90066 (310) 859-5804.

APPENDIX D

COMPULSIVE DOING SURVEY

This survey is intended to assist in increasing understanding of compulsive behavior, its process, and its connection to stressful life events, health, and social problems. Your assistance in completing this survey is very much appreciated! Please include a copy of your ODIST test results if possible.

In order to maintain your anonymity, please do not put your name on this survey when sending it to us. You have premission to photocopy or otherwise reproduce this survey, or you may simply tear out these last pages and mail them to the address below. Your assistance in distributing this survey as widely as possible is appreciated. (To this end, it is suggested that you consider making a copy before sending in your personal results.) Thank you!

Date: _____

First, Middle & Last Initials: _____

What city and state are you from? _____

Are you (check one):
☐ Single   ☐ Married   ☐ Living with someone

How long have you been single, married, or living with someone?
_____

How may children do you have? _____

What are their ages? _____

Have you ever been divorced? ☐ Yes ☐ No

What is your level of education?
☐ High School diploma   ☐ Bachelor's Degree
☐ Associate's Degree   ☐ Professional school
☐ Master's Degree   ☐ Doctorate

What is your occupation? (If you hold more than one job, please indicate all positions.) _____
_____

How satisfied are you with your occupation?
     1   2   3   4   5   6   7
Low   Moderate   High

What is your approximate income? _____

How many hours per week do you work? _____

How many hours per week do you spend playing, relaxing, or doing "nothing"? _____

How satisfied are you with your current lifestyle?
     1   2   3   4   5   6   7
Low   Moderate   High

What was your ODIST score? (We *must* have this for the survey!) _____

Are you involved in counseling, group therapy, or a 12-step group?

☐ Yes (Please describe) _____

☐ No

How would you describe your level of do-aholism?

1	2	3	4	5	6	7
Low			Moderate			High

Please indicate the characteristics of compulsive doing with which you most identify (Check all that apply)

☐ Long work hours   ☐ No rest, recreation, relaxation
☐ Fear of rejection   ☐ Less social life due to doing
☐ Always "shoulding"   ☐ Can't seem to slow down
☐ Impatient, irritable   ☐ Neglecting personal needs
☐ Always being active   ☐ Controlling/caretaking
☐ Perfectionism   ☐ Controlled by externals
☐ Always "forcing"
☐ Other (describe) _____

Would you consider the organization you work for to be work addicted?

☐ Yes   ☐ No   ☐ Maybe

How would you describe your organization's level of work addiction?

1	2	3	4	5	6	7
Low			Moderate			High

Please answer the following in as few words as possible:

A. Three "signs" that your organization is work addicted:
   1. _____
   2. _____
   3. _____
B. Three ways your compulsive doing has impacted your family:

    1. _____
    2. _____
    3. _____
C. Three ways you most often use to recover from your doing
    addiction:
    1. _____
    2. _____
    3. _____

Have you experienced any of the following symptoms, events or
conditions in the past 12 months? (Check all that apply)

☐ High blood pressure ☐ Heart Disease
☐ Sleep problems   ☐ Stomach problems
☐ Frequent headaches   ☐ Low back pain
☐ Frequent illness   ☐ Depression
☐ Frequent accidents   ☐ Frequent errors
☐ Physical tension   ☐ Low self-esteem
☐ Frequent confusion   ☐ Frequent absences from work
☐ Weight gain/loss   ☐ Marital problems
☐ High anxiety   ☐ Restlessness
☐ Sexual problems   ☐ Irritability
☐ Feeling cynical   ☐ Forgetfulness
☐ Agitation   ☐ Complaining
☐ Allergies   ☐ Arthritis
☐ Breathing problems   ☐ Skin problems
☐ Fatigue   ☐ Mood swings
☐ Hopelessness   ☐ Problems with kids
☐ Temper outbursts   ☐ Distractibility
☐ No enjoyment   ☐ Loss of identity

How would you describe your level of general life stress?

    1   2   3   4   5   6   7
Low   Moderate   High

Place an "X" in the box which best describes your family when groing up:

	Disengaged	Separated	Connected	Enmeshed
Chaotic				
Flexible				
Structured				
Rigid				

NOTE: The above chart is adapted from the Circumplex Model in *Circumplex Model: Systemic Assessment and Treatment of Families* by David H. Olsen, Ph.D.

Would you like additional information about programs for compulsive doers?

☐ Yes   ☐ No

WHEN COMPLETED PLEASE MAIL TO:
POWER OF BEING SURVEY
P.O. BOX 6025
GRAND RAPIDS, MI 49516-6025

REFERENCES AND BIBLIOGRAPHY

* *Indicates highly recommended reading similar to THE POWER OF BEING.*

Alcoholics Anonymous (1976). New York: A.A. World Services

American Psychiatric Association (1987). *Diagnostic and Statistical Manual of Mental Disorders, Third Edition, Revised.* Washington, D.C.: American Psychiatric Association.

Anonymous (1990). *The 12 Steps for Everyone.* Minneapolis: Compcare Publishers.

Bastiaans, J. (1968). "Psychoanalytic Investigations on the Psychic Aspects of Acute Myocardial Infarction". *Psychotherapy and Psychosomatics.* 1968, Vol 16(4.-5). Netherlands: University of Leyden.

Beattie, M. (1990). *The Language of Letting Go — Daily Meditations for Co-Dependents.* San Francisco: Harper and Row.

Beattie, M. (1990). *A Co-Dependant's Guide to the 12 Steps.* New York: Prentice Hall.

Beattie, M. (1987). *Co-Dependent No More.* San Francisco: Harper/Hazelden.

Booth-Kewley, S. & Friedman, H.S. (1987). "Psychological Predictors of Heart Disease: A Quantitative Review". *Psychological Bulletin.* May 1987, Vol 101(3). University of California, Riverside.

Bradshaw, J. (1988). *Healing the Shame That Binds You.* Deerfield Beach, FL: Health Communications, Inc.

Brief, Arthur P., Rude, Dale E. & Rabinowitz, Samuel. (1983). "The Impact of Type A Behavior Pattern on Subjective Work Load and Depression". *Journal of Occupational Behavior.* April 1983, Vol 4(2). 157-164.

Brownmiller, S. (1984). *Femininity.* New York: Fawcett.

Brown, L.R. (1990). *The State of the World.* New York: W.W. Norton and Company.

Burke, Ronald J. (1985). "Career Orientations and Type A Behavior in Police Officers". Downsview, Canada.

Capacchione, L. (1979). *The Creative Journal: The Art of Finding Yourself.* Swallow Press/Ohio University Press.

Carnes, P. (1989). *A Gentle Path Through The 12 Steps.* Minneapolis: Compcare Publishers.

Carnes, P. (1983). *Out of the Shadows.* Minneapolis: Compcare Publishers.

Carnes, P. (1989). *Contrary to Love.* Minneapolis: Compcare Publishers.

Castine, J. (1989). *Recovery from Rescuing.* Deerfield Beach, FL: Health Communications, Inc.

Cermak, T.L. (1986). *Diagnosing and Treating Co-Dependence.* Minneapolis: Johnson Institute Books.

Clarke, J.I. & Dawson, C. (1989). *Growing Up Again: Parenting Ourselves and Our Children.* Minneapolis: Hazelden Educational Materials.

Cousins, N. (1989). *Head First: The Biology of Hope.* New York: E.P. Dutton.

Crum, T. (1987). *The Magic of Conflict.* New York: Simon and Schuster, Inc.

Damos, Diane L. (1985). "The Relation Between Type A Behavior Pattern, Pacing, and Subjective Workload Under Single- and Dual-Task Conditions". *Human Factors*. December 1985, Vol 27(6). 675-680. Los Angeles, California: University of Southern California.

Damos, Diane L. & Bloem, Kathryn A. (1985). "Type A Behavior Pattern, Multiple-Task Performance, and Subjective Estimation of Mental Workload". *Bulletin of the Psychonomic Society*. January 1985, Vol 23(1). 53-56. Arizone State University.

Davis, M., McKay, M., & Eshelman, E.R. (1982). *The Relaxation and Stress Reduction Handbook*. Oakland, CA: New Harbinger Publications.

DeSaint-Exupery, A. (1943). *The Little Prince*. New York: Harcourt, Brace and World, Inc.

Dougherty, S. (1989). "Analysis of a Selected Number of Female Workaholics". *Dissertation*. December 1989, Vol 50(6-A). Washingtonn, D.C.: George Washington University.

Ecker, R.E. (1985). *The Stress Myth*. Downers Grove, IL: InterVarsity Press.

Ellis, A. (1983). "My Philosophy of Work and Love." *Psychotherapy in Private Practice*. Spring 1983, Vol 1(1). New York, NY: Institute for Rational-Emotive Therapy.

Erikson, E.H. (1963). *Childhood and Society*. New York: W.W. Norton & Company.

Eschholz, P. & Rosa, A. (1987). *Outlooks and Insights*. New York: St. Martin's Press, Inc.

Fassel, D. (1990) *Working Ourselves to Death: The High Cost of Workaholism and the Rewards of Recovery*. New York: Harper and Row.

*Fassel, D. (1990) *Working Ourselves to Death - The High Cost of Workaholism and the Rewards of Recovery.* New York: Harper Collins.

Fields, R. (1984). *Chop Wood, Carry Water.* New York: Jeremy P. Tarcher.

Fossum, M. (1989). *Catching Fire: Men's Renewal and Recovery Through Crisis.* Mineapolis: Hazelden Foundation.

Friel, J. & Friel, L. (1988). *Adult Children: The Secrets of Dysfunctional Families.* Deerfield Beach, FL: Health Communications, Inc.

Friel, J. & Friel, L. (1990). *An Adult Child's Guide to What's "Normal".* Deerfield Beach, FL: Health Communications, Inc.

Froggatt, Kirk L. & Cotton, John L. "The Impact of Type A Behavior Pattern on Overload-Induced Stress and Performance Attributions". *Journal of Management.* Spring 1987, Vol 13(1). 87-98.

Furnham, Adrian F. (1990). "The Protestant Work Ethic and Type A Behaviour: A Pilot Study. England.

Gibran, K. (1923). *The Prophet.* New York: Alfred A. Knopf Publishers.

Guyton, A.C. (1977). *Basic Human Psychology.* Second Edition, Philadelphia: Saunders.

Halvorson, R. & Deilgar, V. (1989). *The 12 Steps — A Way Out: A Working Guide for Adult Children from Addictive and Other Dysfunctional Families.* Revised Edition, Recovery SD.

Haas, R. (1989). "Workaholism: A Conceptual View and Development of a Measurement Instrument" *Dissertation.* November 1989, Vol 50(5-B). United States International University.

Helldorfer, M.C. (1987). "Church Professionals and Work Addiction". *Studies in Formative Spirituality*. May 1987, Vol 8(2). Middletown, CT: House of Affirmation, Consultation Center.

* Hemfelt, Dr. R., Minirth, Dr. F., Meier, Dr. P. (1982). *We Are Driven — The Compulsive Behaviors America Aplauds*. Nashville, TN: Thomas Nelson.

Hollander, J. (1990). *How to Make the World a Better Place*. New York: William Morrow.

Homer, J. (1985). "Worker Burnout: A Dynamic Model with Implications for Prevention and Control". *System Dynamics Review*. Summer, 1985, Vol 1(1). Los Angeles, CA: University of Southern California.

Hurrell, Joseph J. "Machine-Paced Work and the Type A Behaviour Pattern". *Journal of Occupational Psychology*. March 1985, Vol 58(1). 15-25. Cincinnati, Ohio.

Janas, C. (1987). "Seeking Magical Solutions, Exploring Addictions". *Medical Hypnoanalysis Journal*. March 1987, Vol 2(1).

John-Roger & McWilliams, P. (1991). *Life 101*. New York: Bantam Books

Joseph, B. (1985). "Process Communication Management: The Micro Chip of the O.D. World". *Organization Development Journal*. Fall 1985, Vol 3(3). Lakewood, OH: Taibi Kahler Associates.

* Keyes, R. (1991). *Timelock — How Life Got So Hectic and What You Can Do About It*. New York: Harper Collins.

*Kinder, Dr. M. (1990) *Going Nowhere Fast — Step Off Life's Treadmills and Find Peace of Mind.* New York: Ballantine Books.

Kirmeyer, Sandra L. (1988). "Coping with Competing Demands: Interruption and the Type A Pattern". *Journal of Applied Psychology.* November 1988, Vol 73(4) 621-629. Columbia, Missouri: University of Missouri.

Komor, C. (1982). *The Relationship of Life Stress and Physiological Illness Among Undergraduate College Students.* San Diego: Christian Komor.

* Komor, C., Psy.D. (1991). *The Power of Being — For People Who Do Too Much.* Grand Rapids, MI: Renegade House Productions.

Kritsberg, W. (1990). *Healing Together: A Guide to Intimacy and Recovery for Co-Dependent Couples.* Deerfield Beach, FL: Health Communications, Inc.

Kushnir, T. & Melamed, S. (1991). "Work-Load, Perceived Control and Psychological Distress in Type A/B Industrial Workers". *Journal of Organizational Behavior.* March 1991, Vol 12(2) 155-168. Ra'annana, Israel: Lowenstien Hospital.

LaoTzu (1944). *The Way of Life.* New York: Perigee Books.

Larrange, R. (1990). *Calling It A Day — Daily Meditations for Workaholics.* New York: Harper and Row.

Larson, E. (1985). *Stage Two Recovery: Life Beyond Addiction.* New York: W.W. Norton and Company.

Machlowitz, M. (1979). "Determining the Effects of Workaholism". *Dissertation.* July 1979, Vol 40(1-B). Yale University.

Machlowitz, M. (1980). *Workaholics*. Reading, MA: Addison-Wesley.

McGoldrick, M. & Gersen, R. (1985). *Genograms in Family Assessment*. New York: W.W. Norton and Company.

McKay, M., David, M., & Fanning, P. (1981). *Thoughts and Feelings: The Art of Cognitive Stress Intervention*. Oakland, CA: New Harbinger Publications.

Milkman, H. & Sunderwirth, S. (1987). *Craving for Ecstasy*. Lexington, MA: D.C. Heath and Company.

* Miller, J. K. (1987). *Hope in the Fast Lane*. New York: Harper Collins.

* Minirth, F.; Meier, P.; Wichern, F.; Brewer, B.; Skipper, S. (1981) *The Workaholic and His Family — An Inside Look*. Grand Rapids, MI: Baker Book House Company.

* Minirth, F., M.D.; Hawkins, D., Th.M.; Meier, P., M.D.; Flournoy, R., Ph.D. *How To Beat Burnout - Help for Men and Women*. Illinois: The Moody Bible Institute of Chicago.

Nagy, S. & Davis, L.G. (1985). "Burnout: A Comparitive Analysis of Personality and Environmental Variables". *Psychological Reports*. December 1985, Vol 57(3, pt 2). University of Alabama.

Napier, A.Y. (1988). *The Fragile Bond*. New York: Harper and Row.

Naughton, T. (1987). "A Conceptual View of Workaholism and Implications for Career Counseling and Research". *Career Development*

Quarterly. March 1987, Vol 35(3). Detroit, MI: Wayne State University.

Newton, Tim J. & Keenan, Tony. (1990). "The Moderating Effect of the Type A Behavior Pattern and Locus of Control Upon the Relationship Between Change in Job Demands and Change in Psychological Strain". *Human Relations.* December 1990, Bol 43(12). 1229-1255. Scotland: University of Edinburgh.

Orth-Gomer, Kristina & Unden, Anna Lena. (1990). "Type A Behavior, Social Support, and Coronary Risk: Interaction and Significance of Mortality in Cardiac Patients". *Psychosomatic Medicine.* January-February 1990, Vol 52(1). 59-772. Stockholm, Sweden.

Osbon, D.K. (1991). *Reflections On The Art of Living: A Joseph Campbell Companion.* New York: Harper Collins

Ottenberg, P. (1975). "The Physician's Disease: Success and Work Addiction". *Psychiatric Opinion.* April 1975, Vol 12(4). Philadelphia, PA: Private Practice.

Overbeck, T.J. (1976). "The Workaholic". *Psychology.* August 1979, Bol 13(3). University of Santa Clara Jesuit Conmunity.

Pace, L.A. (1988). "Addictive Type-A Behavior Undermines Employee Involvement". *Personnel Journal.* June 1988, Vol 67(6). Webster, NY: Xerox Corporation.

Paulley, J.W. (1975). "Cultural Influences on the Incidence and Pattern of Disease". *Psychotherapy and Psychosomatics.* 1975, Bol 26(1). England: Ipswich Hospital.

Paulus, T. (1972). *Hope for the Flowers*. New York: Paulist Press.

Penzer, W.N. (1984). "The Psychopathology of the Psychotherapist". *Psychotherapy in Private Practice*. Summer, 1984, Vol 2(2). Plantation, FL: Private Practice.

Peters, T.J. & Austin, N.K. (1989). *A Passion for Excellence*. Warner Books

Peterson, A.V. (1982). "Pathogram: A Visual Aid to Obtain Focus and Commitment". *Journal of Reality Therapy*. Fall 1982, Vol 2(1). Texas: Texas Technological University.

Pietropinto, A. (1986). "The Workaholic Spouse". *Medical Aspects of Human Sexuality*. May 1986, Vol 20(5). New York, NY: Cabrini Medical Center.

Riley, M. (1990). *Corporate Healing: Solutions to the Impact of the Addictive Personality in the Workplace*. Deerfield Beach, FL: Health Communications, Inc.

* Robinson, B. (1989). *Work Addiction: Hidden Legacies of Adult Children*. Deerfield Beach, FL: Health Communications, Inc.

Robinson, B. (1990). *Soothing Moments: Daily Meditaions for Fast-Track Living*. Deerfield Beach, FL: Health Communications, Inc.

* Robinson, B. (1992). *Overdoing It: How to Slow Down and Take Care of Yourself*. Deerfield Beach, FL: Health Communications, Inc.

Rohrlich, J. (1980). *Work and Love: The Crucial Balance*.

Rohrlich, J. (1981). "The Dynamics of Work Addiction". *Israel Journal of Psychiatry and*

Related Sciences. 1981, Vol 18(2). New York: Cornell University.

Schaef, A. & Fassel, D. (1988). *The Addictive Organization.* San Francisco: Harper and Row.

Schaef, A. (1986). *Women's Reality: An Emerging Female System in the White Male Society.* New York: Harper and Row.

Schaef, A. (1987). *When Society Becomes An Addict.* New York: Harper and Row.

* Schor, J.B. (1991) *The Overworked American — The Unexpected Decline of Leisure.* New York: Basic Books

Seiler, R.E. (1984-85). "Dysfunctional Stress Among University Faculty". *Educational Research Quarterly.* 1984-85, Vol 9(2). Houston: University of Houston.

Shostrom, E. (1967). *Man, the Manipulator.* New York, Bantam Books.

Siegal, B. (1986). *Love, Medicine and Miracles.* New York: Harper and Row.

Sinetar, M. (1989). *Do What You Love: The Money Will Follow: Discover Your Right Livelihood.* Dell Trade Publishers.

Sorensen, Glorian & Jacobs, David R. (1987). "Relationships Among Type A Behavior, Employment Experiences, and Gender: The Minnesota Heart Survey". *Journal of Behavioral Medicine.* August 1987, Vol 10(4). 323-336. Worcester, Massachusetts: University of Massachusetts Medical School.

Sprankle, J. & Ebel, H. (1987). *The Workaholic Syndrome: Your Job Is Not Your Life* Walker and Company.

Spruell, G. (1987). "Work Fever". *Training and Development Journal.* January 1987, Vol 41(1). Alexandria, VA: American Society for Training and Development.

Subby, R.C. (1987). *Lost in the Shuffle.* Deerfield Beach, FL: Health Communications, Inc.

Subby, R.C. (1990). *Healing the Family.* Deerfield Beach, FL: Health Communications, Inc.

Tohei, K. (1980). *Ki In Daily Life.* Toyko, Ki No Kenkyukai H.Q.

Westman, M., Eden, D., & Shirom, A. (1985). "Job Stress, Cigarette Smoking and Cessation: The Conditioning Effects of Peer Support". *Social Science and Medicine.* 1985, Vol 20(6). Ramat-Aviv, Israel: Tel-Aviv University.

Wholey, D. (1988). *Becoming Your Own Parent.* New York: Doubleday.

Williams, P. (1987). *Remember Your Essence.* New York: Harmony Books.

Winokur, J. (1989). *Zen To Go.* New York: Penguin Books.

Woititz, J.G. (1983). *Adult children of Alcoholics.* Deerfield Beach, FL: Health Communications, Inc.

Woititz, J.G. (1985). *Struggle for Intimacy.* Deerfield Beach, FL: Health Communications, Inc.

Woititz, J.G. (1987). *Home Away From Home: The Art of Self-Sabatoge.* Deerfield Beach, FL: Health Communications, Inc.

Woodside, M. (1986). *Children of Alcoholics On the Job.*

Dr. Christian R. Komor

ABOUT THE AUTHOR

Christian R. Komor, Psy.D. is a licensed psychologist and career psychotherapist currently in private practice in Grand Rapids, Michigan. *The Power of Being: For People Who Do Too Much* is a synthesis of Chris' long-standing interest in the treatment of stress-related psychological problems, personal growth, and in our society's approach to work. Chris lives with his wife and dog and now does much of his writing in a hammock on his front porch.

Dr. Christian R. Komor

The Power of Being

ORDER BLANK

Please send materials selected below to (please print):

Name: _____

Street: _____ Apt.# _____

City: _____ State: _____ Zip _____

Phone (_____) _____

____ **"The Power of Being: For People Who Do Too Much"** by Dr. Christian R. Komor ($10.95 each) In our society, we often do too much. This book provides a means for understanding and healing from compulsive behaviors such as: over-working, perfectionism, and "shoulding". Includes 70 ideas for personal healing and recovery. (275 pages)

____ **"Over Doing It Screening Test (ODIST)"** ($3.50 each) Based on the research for "The Power of Being", the ODIST provides individuals with an opportunity to assess the degree to which compulsive work behavior is present in their life. The test is self-scoring and includes a general description of compulsive doing. (6 pages)

____ **"A.S.S.E.N.T. Into Health"** ($3.50 each) Outline and accompanying descriptions of a comprehensive and unique stress management program including the basic ways in which stress impacts us in daily life. Areas included in the program include: Attitude, Sleep, Support Systems, Exercise, Nutrition, and Time Management. (3 pages)

____ Please send me **information** on presentations and workshops on personal growth, stress management, and workaholism. (no charge)

Add $2.00 for Shipping and Handling

Total Enclosed: $_____

Please make check/money order payable to:
Renegade House Productions, P.O. Box 6025, Grand Rapids, Michigan 49516-6025 (616) 956-7905.
Credit Card Orders: (800) 444-2524
Thank you!